"*20 Life-Transforming Choices Adoptees Need to Make* is indeed life-transforming for those who will take advantage of the wisdom contained therein. The practical help given in chapters six and seven alone are worth the price of the book! So often as adoptees we can struggle with a lack of understanding from those who are not adopted, and how to respond to triggering statements or actions. Sherrie's wisdom on these issues is spot on. Adoptees will find great solace in her words and real help for the plethora of issues we deal with post-adoption. I am so very grateful for this amazing resource!"

—*Deanna Doss Shrodes, Blogger, Adoptee Restoration and Author of* Worthy to Be Found

"As an adoptive mom and singer/songwriter and speaker at adoption conferences, I am once again VERY grateful for the honest and extremely helpful nature of Sherrie's latest book, *20 Life-Transforming Choices Adoptees Need to Make*. Her previous books have been instrumental in preparing me and assisting us after the fact in our own family's adoption of two siblings who'd suffered greatly. As our children grow and comprehend more of their past, present, and future, Sherrie's insights and significant research continue to be an indispensable part of the healing, understanding, and hope-inspiring process for our entire family."

—*Becky Wright, Singer/Songwriter/Speaker, Founder of Tahlequah Orphan & Adoption Ministries, Department of Artists in Christian Testimony International*

"Sherrie Eldridge, the adoption expert who has so ably helped adoptive parents better understand their children's needs, is back again, helping other adoptees to learn from her own journey through search and reunion with her latest guide, *20 Life-Transforming Choices Adoptees Need to Make*. It's a well-written guide for adoptees of all ages, empowering them to grow in positive new directions—regardless of the outcome of their search. If adoption is your mountain, Sherrie Eldridge is your best possible sherpa, for few understand all of its peaks and passes the way Sherrie does, and her sage advice can help you reach your

—*El_____ _____C, LMFT*
Exe_____ ssociatesa

"This is a powerfully written book. Sherrie's revealing documentation of her insights for adoptees combined with her own and others' intimate, personal experiences dramatically highlight her difficult but liberating journey."

—*Dale E. Theobald, Ph.D., M.D., Senior Medical Director for Community Home Health Services and Palliative Care at Community North Health Network, Indianapolis, Indiana*

"Although geared toward adoptee concerns and beliefs, Sherrie Eldridge's latest book provides practical and spiritual information helpful to both adoptive and birth families. Social workers, therapists, and adoption professionals will find this book an important companion piece to Ms. Eldridge's first book, *20 Things Adopted Kids Wish Their Adoptive Parents Knew.*"

—*Dirck Brown, Ed.D., Author of* Clinical Practice in Adoption *and Founder of Post Adoption Center for Education and Research (PACER)*

"Sherrie Eldridge speaks what so many of us wish we'd been able to explain to our adoptive parents. This has helped me tremendously as an adoptive mother myself now."

—*Rebecca Kiessling, Founder and President of Save The 1, Co-Founder of Hope After Rape Conception, International Speaker and Attorney, Adoptee and Adoptive Mother*

"It is impossible to articulate how life-changing Sherrie Eldridge's book has been for me! This book gave voice to my thoughts, emotions, and actions that were holding me back from fully living the life I was created to live. Eldridge uncovers the common threads adoptees hold on to throughout our lives, including grief, loss, rejection, fear, hope and love. Many clients say, 'I wish I had known about this resource years ago.'"

—*LeAnne Parsons CPC, ELI-MP, The Walk Your Talk Coach, Legacy Now Lived*™

20 LIFE-TRANSFORMING CHOICES ADOPTEES

Need to Make

SECOND EDITION

by the same author

Forever Fingerprints
An Amazing Discovery for Adopted Children
Sherrie Eldridge
ISBN 978 1 84905 778 3
eISBN 978 1 78450 021 4

of related interest

Healing from Loss After Adoption or Foster Care
A Guide for Adults
Renée Wolfs
Foreword by Marlene van Steensel
Translated by Kate Eaton
ISBN 978 1 84905 555 0
eISBN 978 0 85700 988 3

Building Self-Esteem in Children and Teens
Who Are Adopted or Fostered
Dr. Sue Cornbluth
Foreword by Nyleen Shaw
ISBN 978 1 84905 466 9
eISBN 978 0 85700 844 2

Reparenting the Child Who Hurts
A Guide to Healing Developmental Trauma and Attachments
Caroline Archer and Christine Gordon
Foreword by Gregory C. Keck, Ph.D.
ISBN 978 1 84905 263 4
eISBN 978 0 85700 568 7

20

LIFE-
TRANSFORMING
CHOICES
ADOPTEES
Need to Make

—— SECOND EDITION ——

Sherrie Eldridge

Jessica Kingsley *Publishers*
London and Philadelphia

The poem "Caring Enough to Hear and Be Heard" by David Augsburger, on page 121 is reproduced with kind permission of Baker Publishing Group. The poem "They Said" by Mi Ok Song Bruining on page 79 is reproduced with kind permission of the author. The poem "Pandora in Later Life" on page 63 is reproduced with kind permission of the author. Excerpt from the W.I.S.E. UP! Program on pages 102–7 is reproduced with kind permission of Debbie B. Riley of the Centre for Adoption Support and Education. Unless otherwise identified, all Scripture quotations in this publication are taken from the Holy Bible: New Iinternational Version® (NIV®). Copyright © 1973, 1978, 1984 by International Bible Society. Used by permission of Zondervan Publishing House. All rights reserved. Other versions used include: the New American Standard Bible (NASB), © The Lockman Foundation 1960, 1962, 1963, 1968, 1971, 1972, 1973, 1975, 1977; The Message: New Testament with Psalms and Proverbs by Eugene H. Peterson, copyright © 1993, 1994, 1995, used by permission of NavPress Publishing Group.

Every effort has been made to trace copyright holders and to obtain their permission for the use of copyright material. The author and the publisher apologize for any omissions and would be grateful if notified of any acknowledgements that should be incorporated in future reprints or editions of this book.

First edition published by Piñon Press in 2003
Second edition first published in 2015
by Jessica Kingsley Publishers
73 Collier Street
London N1 9BE, UK
and
400 Market Street, Suite 400
Philadelphia, PA 19106, USA

www.jkp.com

Copyright © Sherrie Eldridge 2003, 2015

Author photo: Tom Rockwell

Some of the anecdotal illustrations in this book are true to life and are included with the permission of the persons involved. Some names have been changed to protect privacy. All other illustrations are composites of real situations, and any resemblance to people living or dead is coincidental.

This publication is designed to provide accurate and authoritative information in regard to the subject matter covered. It is sold with the understanding that the author and the publisher are not engaged in rendering legal, accounting, or other professional service. If legal advice or other expert assistance is required, the services of a competent professional person should be sought. From a Declaration of Principles jointly adopted by a Committee of the American Bar Association and a Committee of Publishers.

Library of Congress Cataloging in Publication Data
Eldridge, Sherrie.
  Twenty life transforming choices adoptees need to make / Sherrie Eldridge. -- Second Edition.
    pages cm
  Originally published: Colorado Springs, Colo. : Pinon Press, c2003.
  Includes bibliographical references.
  ISBN 978-1-84905-774-5 (alk. paper)
  1. Adoptees--Psychology. 2. Adoption--Psychological aspects. I. Title.
  HV875.E383 2015
  362.82'98--dc23
                        2014037466

British Library Cataloguing in Publication Data
A CIP catalogue record for this book is available from the British Library

ISBN 978 1 84905 774 5
eISBN 978 1 78450 017 7

Printed and bound in the United States

To my husband, Bob, who has loved me well.

CONTENTS

PART TWO: TWENTY TRUTHS AND TWENTY CHOICES THAT CAN TRANSFORM

ACKNOWLEDGMENTS

This book is due to the incredible talents and contributions of:

- Steve Jones, Acquisitions Editor for Jessica Kingsley Publishers, for enthusiastically launching this second edition.

- Rita Rosenkranz, the best literary agent anyone could ask for.

- Bob Eldridge, who freed me up in a multitude of ways for writing.

Thanks to contributing adoptees and friends, for sharing your hearts so that others know they are not alone:

Shefalie Chandra, Tiffany Williams Savage, Deana Doss Shrodes, Rebecca Kiessling, Shirley A. Reynolds, Joy Budensiek, Sheila Rounds, Kim Norman, Laurie, Maggie Backiewicz, Sharon McGowan, Joe Soll, Scott D. Stephens, Penny Callan Partridge, Paula Oliver, Pam Hasegawa, Phyllis-Anne Munro, Kimberly Steiner, Sandy Garrett, Ron Hilliard, Richard B. Gilbert, Connie Dawson, Renee Mills, Greg Berger, Michelle Van Keulen, Deborah Anne Rainey, Richard Curtis, Frieda

Moore, Cheri Freeman, Sharon Partridge, Susan Coons, Dirck Brown, Lois Rabey, Carol Peterson, Bob Blanchard, Dawn Saphir, Michelle Chance, Stephanie Ericksen, Derek Jeske, Rebecca L. Ricardo, Teresa Armor, Janet Carnright, Kasey Hamner, Jody Moreen, Melinda Faust, Erika Hill, Paige Wilson, Kenny Tucker, Robbin Puckett, Amy Abramson, Judith Roberts, Carolyn Halliburton, Karen Stinger, Emmary Nicholson, Sue Drese, Trish DePew, Rick Ennis, Viorel Badescu, Deb Wood, Cheri Manternach, Lori Ann Pewsey, Jodi Strathman, Cheri Manternach, Issie, Vicky Rockwell, and countless others.

part ONE

Our Lifelong Search For Truth

How you choose to respond to each moment of the movie of life determines how you see the next frame, and the next, and eventually how you feel when the movie ends.

—DOC CHILDRE

CHAPTER one

Caught Unaware

Why would a forty-seven-year-old woman, who, from all outward appearances, "had it all", risk re-experiencing what once had caused her deep feelings of abandonment and loss?

Why would she become one of the growing numbers of adoptees who search for their birth families?

Why would she venture on such a quest, even after most family members and friends advised against it?

Why would she write numerous letters to a judge in the county where she was born, requesting birth information that had been sealed, for decades?

Why?

Because she heard the song of the nightingale. That quiet voice. The voice that sings ever so softly, ever so gently, usually in the dark times of life, and particularly on birthdays.

I am this woman.

Reflecting back, adoption was like a door with a peephole: the only times I peeked through it were when somebody asked my nationality or when I had to fill in a medical form. I said the words all adoptees detest: "I don't know…I was adopted."

My parents told me I was adopted at a young age, but that was it. It wasn't mentioned again.

Years later, when my husband Bob and I were expecting our first child, I read the little brochures in the obstetrician's office about how the baby develops every month. Then came the first sign of life, that little kick from the inside. There was the final push in delivery and then the scream of the first blood relative in my life, my newborn daughter Lisa. With strawberry-colored peach fuzz hair and rosy cheeks, she was bone of my bone and flesh of my flesh.

Two years later, when pregnant with our second daughter at age twenty-two, I wondered, *How could a woman carry a baby for nine months and not worry about it every day?* I loved my sweet new baby, Chrissie, and couldn't imagine handing her over to someone else.

Did my birth mother wonder about my development when she carried me? Did she feel wonderfully strange when she saw her bulging tummy? What was it like for her when she was carrying me? Did she thrill when she felt me kick from the inside? Did she see me after my birth?

These questions flung wide open the issue of my adoption.

I wanted to find my birth mother and tell her not to feel guilty, because I had good parents and a happy upbringing. I searched quietly while bringing up our daughters, and kept my curiosity at bay with perfectionism. Super mom. Super executive wife. Super friend. The whole bit.

And so, life went on. The kids grew up, went to college, and got married.

At age forty, I was at a convention, and I'd had to sign up ahead of time for the seminars I wanted to attend. When I got to the seminar of my choice, it was packed, with no seating available. Disappointed, I searched for another seminar and discovered one where an attractive, animated, middle-aged woman was saying from the podium, "My life was changed forever."

There were seats available, so I quietly slipped in. As I settled into my chair, the speaker started using words and phrases like "birth mother" and "give up for adoption." Those words hadn't entered my head since I was a young mother. Tapping my pen, I took a deep breath.

It wasn't long before I figured out that the speaker was a birth mother. Apparently she'd had a date with a colleague who was hosting a party at his home. When she arrived, she waited expectantly for the other guests to arrive. Minutes turned into hours as she came to the frightening realization that there wasn't going to be a party. Instead, she had been set up for something that would mar her life forever—violent rape, resulting in pregnancy. As she neared her delivery date, she made an "agonizing decision" to place her baby for adoption, believing she would never see her again.

For the finale of her presentation, she told a poignant story of how the infant daughter she had relinquished found her twenty-three years later. With a radiant smile, she held up a huge, close-up photo of their faces. It was amazing. Same color of hair. Same eyes. Same smile. They looked exactly alike!

After the seminar, I walked out into the noisy crowd, oblivious to the chatter, as if a veil had fallen over me, and inside that veil a new thought pounded my consciousness: *I wonder if I look like my birth mother.*

I had been caught unaware by this woman's story of reunion and redemption.

Facing loss once more

A few months later I visited my eighty-three-year-old father in my hometown of St. Johns, Michigan. That evening Dad pulled out the old rusty, steel file box that was to provide all the information I needed when he was gone.

I could see it coming, like a freight train bustling down a track. I knew what he was doing; he was preparing for death and wanted me to be prepared as well.

The thought of losing him was unbearable. I hadn't allowed myself to even go there in my thoughts until then. Mom had been dead for eleven long years, and because I was an only child, my father's impending death would leave me without a family. I would be an orphan once more. How I dreaded that reality.

Dad sorted through the papers with his gnarly fingers and age-spotted hands. When he came to a folded, yellowed document, he said, "I haven't seen this in a long time."

"What is it?" I asked.

"Your adoption certificate."

"My adoption certificate?" I gasped. "The *original*? Can I see it?"

As he handed over the document, he sighed deeply, reached across the table, and grabbed my hand. "I still remember the day your grandmother brought you through the front door. You were so tiny! I could hold you in the palm of my hand! Your mom and I came running from the kitchen to welcome you home. We were so happy."

I choked back tears. My dad's mom, Leah Cook, had been the dedicated case worker who arranged my adoption. She was a woman ahead of her time.

As I opened the document, my eyes were riveted on four simple words: Mother: Marjorie Elizabeth Perry.

Oh, my goodness!

"Why didn't anybody ever tell me my birth mother's name?" I asked.

Dad thought I had known it all along. I didn't press him any further because I was afraid that the kindling interest in my birth mother might hurt him.

Memories about what my late mother had told me about my adoption came to mind. *Your dad was an executive at GM in Flint. If you ever want to be rich, look him up. Your mother worked for your dad. The physician who delivered you was Dr. Miles Fillinger from Ovid.*

Something changed the night Dad pulled out the adoption papers. Through my adoption door I could see a woman. And not just *any* woman. This woman was my *birth* mother, with a *real* name and address.

The "A" word

I couldn't wait for Dad to go to bed so that I could look in the local phone book to see if she lived nearby.

After good-night kisses, I tucked the little phone book with the yellow plastic cover under my bathrobe and went to my bedroom at the back of the house. As I sat on the edge of the bed, my sweaty hands turned page after page. *Perry.* Was there anyone by that name in nearby Ovid? No. In the little burg of Fowler? No. Well, how about St. Johns? No, there were none.

I tossed and turned all night. The moon peeking through the well-worn, green curtains made just enough light for me to stare at the plaster swirls in the ceiling. I remembered sleepless nights during childhood. I must have dozed off just before dawn.

I awakened to the sound and smell of fresh coffee brewing in the kitchen. Dad was already up, barefoot and dressed in a slightly soiled white terrycloth robe tied loosely around his waist. How I loved that knotty pine kitchen with the yellow Formica counter tops and Mom's framed needlepoint designs… especially the one of the ladybug. This had been my home, my haven, since I was adopted at ten days old.

As always I gave Dad a good-morning hug and kiss. We ate our usual bowl of Wheaties as he gave me fatherly instructions to be careful driving home to Indiana. And then it was time to say goodbye. How I hated to say goodbye, for I never knew when it would be the last time.

As I pulled out of his gravel driveway, Dad, still in his bathrobe, stood waving at the doorway of the screened-in porch. Tears welled up, big time.

I headed up Oakland Street, the tree-lined street that had such prestige only a few decades ago. I drove as if heading for Indiana, but when I was out of Dad's sight, I turned toward the county courthouse. Surely they would have more information about my birth mother.

I felt very small as I walked the darkened hallways of the courthouse. Those twelve-foot ceilings led toward the county clerk's office. It seemed like an eerie tomb where the identity of my birth mother was buried.

A friendly clerk asked if she could help. I gave her a big smile, introducing myself as an adoptee, wanting information about my birth mother.

Suddenly her neck stiffened. "You will have to make written application to the probate judge for release of any information," she snapped as she handed me a form titled "Non-Identifying Information."

This was my first lesson about searching for birth information. *Never* mention the word "adoptee," for it almost always closes the door for further information. "Genealogical research" is the socially correct term, I later learned.

After returning home I completed and returned the paperwork and haunted the mailbox every day. A few weeks later a form letter arrived:

> I am sorry to inform you that I do not find any consent for release of identifying information from either of your biological parents. As we are prohibited from giving out identifying information without these consents, the following is the only information that can be given at

this time. This data is from your original birth certificate. Date of birth, August 4, 1945, Clinton Memorial Hospital, St. Johns, Michigan, County of Clinton, Time, 5:57 a.m. Pregnancy full term. Parents married. Father, 27 and a sergeant in the US Army. Mother, 21 and a housewife. No other children, living or dead. Parents voluntarily consented to this adoption.

What?

First child? *Married* parents? *Willingly* consented? How could that be? How could a young, married couple with *no* children *willingly* give up their firstborn child? What kind of people were they anyway? It would have been different if they were sixteen and unmarried. That I could understand. But *married*, twenty-one and twenty-seven?

Then one detail caught my attention. "Time [of birth], 5:57 a.m."

Oh, my goodness! *I really was born.* I wasn't an alien who was dropped down into my adoptive parents' arms. I was a *real* baby who experienced a *real* birth from a *real* mother at a *real* time of the day. For me, that tidbit of information was like a meal to a starving woman.

That did it! I had just stepped over the line. There was no turning back now. I *had* to find her, no matter the cost.

I wanted to tell everyone about my plan. It was no longer going to be a secret journey. I wanted everyone in my life to cheer me on.

And did they?

Unfortunately, no.

Bob was afraid I would be hurt and at the least, disappointed. I got up the nerve to tell my elderly dad and he asked why I would want "to open up that can of worms." Some family members were conspicuously quiet. Some people told me I *already* had parents…why would I seek out another mother?

And well-meaning religious people remarked, "Why do that? You already know your identity as a child of God."

Why couldn't people be happy for me?

But there was one person who stood by me all the way—my husband's cousin, Jan. I stayed at her house when the time came to do my actual search in Michigan.

From then on, I was *obsessed* for the next seven years to find a Marjorie Elizabeth Perry in the state of Michigan.

At one point I visited the hospital where I was born to request birth records. Surely they would be able to at least tell me about my birth. I was not aware of any law that prohibited it. I knew enough by then not to mention the "A" word.

The administrator of records came from behind sliding glass office doors into the lobby, sat down next to me, put her hand gently on my knee, and said, "Now, dearie, do we have an adoptee here? I'm sorry, but we can't give out that kind of information to adoptees."

My face flushed. Adrenaline rushed through my veins. It was all I could do to keep from punching her! I felt like a naughty little girl who had just had her hands slapped.

The dreaded event

My dad's health was steadily declining. One day we got a call from the hospital saying that we should come as soon as possible. Did we want life support? Dad and I had already discussed that option so I knew he would want me to tell the doctor no, without any guilt or regret.

Bob, Lisa, and I rushed to his bedside. He was in a coma but roused when he heard his granddaughter's voice. Paul Jopke, his best friend for a lifetime, slipped in at one point. I tried to get Dad to gain consciousness, but Paul gently pulled me away, wrapped his arms around me, and held me as I sobbed. He didn't say a word. He didn't need to.

Within twelve hours Dad was gone. I don't think I have ever cried as hard and long as I did in the days that followed.

The search intensifies

Dad's death intensified my search. Finally, overwhelmed with seven years of failed attempts at finding my mother, I hired an adoption professional, Marian. As I waited for her to arrive for our breakfast appointment at a restaurant on the east side of Lansing, I put on my "I-have-it-all-together" mask, but beneath it was a terrified child.

Before long, a spunky, redheaded, middle-aged woman came bounding through the door. She had been helping others do their searches for years, just out of the goodness of her heart and her love for adoptees.

"What do you think she'll be like…a queen or a bag lady?" she asked.

"Nobody has ever asked me that," I said sheepishly. "Probably a bag lady. I really don't have any positive feelings about her."

In the hours that followed I tagged behind this sleuth as she combed old city directories at the State of Michigan Library, searched death indexes at the Mormon Church, and ordered birth, marriage, and death certificates at the Michigan State Department of Health.

The break came with my biological grandfather's death certificate. The name of the funeral home that took care of his remains was on the certificate. It was in Cheboygan, Michigan.

"We've hit pay dirt!" the intermediary exclaimed, as I tried to figure out what that meant. "Let's both go home and I'll call the funeral home to see if they have any next of kin listed on their records. I'll call you as soon as I find out something."

On the drive back to my hometown of St. Johns, my thoughts turned to my parents. What would they have thought and said about all of this? I decided to stop by the cemetery where they were buried. The wind whipped around me as I walked toward their tombstone. If only I could talk to them. If only I could have one more hug. If only I could hear them say one more time how much they loved me and I could tell them one more time how much I loved them. If only I could tell them that we had found her. Tears spilled down my cheeks as I returned to the car.

Two hours later Marian called to say that she had found my birth mother's current name and address, which was a miracle, for she had remarried twice and moved several times. Marian asked what I wanted her to say to my birth mother. "I want to know my nationality, medical history, and who my father is." At the last moment, I thought about the era in which she carried me to term and couldn't imagine the pain and shame she had endured from family and society. I choked back tears and said, "And tell her 'thank you' for giving me the gift of birth."

An hour later, when the phone rang, I asked if the news was good or bad.

"Both," she said. "Your mother wants you to know that she is a mother you can be proud of. Her voice sounds just like yours! Your heritage is Irish and she knows of no major health problems in the family. However, she doesn't want to talk about your birth father and wants no further contact with you."

Really?

Marian and I talked a few minutes longer and then her "call waiting" signal clicked in. It was my birth mother; she had changed her mind and wanted me to call, with one stipulation: that I not ask about my birth father ever again.

The first contact

A voice that sounded like mine said, "Hello."

"Marjorie?" I said.

"Yes, but everyone calls me Elizabeth," she said and we began talking about trivialities. *What do you look like? How tall are you? Do you have a dimple in your chin?*

I frantically took notes the entire time, not wanting to forget a single detail. I have them to this day years later. Minutes turned into hours as she told me about her successful social and professional life as an interior designer. "Clients used to send their personal jets to pick me up for jobs."

I had always loved interior design. In fact, I almost studied it in college. People tell me I'm good at it. Now I knew where I got the talent. But I kept having to reassure myself, *Sherrie, she's your mother. She's not going to reject you because you are a woman with an unexciting life like hers.* Still, that fear kept popping into my mind.

My mother told me later that she called her priest in the morning and as he listened to her reveal her long-guarded secret (me), he reassured her that I would be a source of blessing.

The next week a hand-addressed envelope came in the mail containing two photos of her. Where was my elation? She looked "hard" and cold. Along with the photos was a note:

> Enclosed are two photos—one taken last week and one when I was nearly your age. I didn't sleep a wink last night, as I'm sure you didn't. Best wishes to your husband and thank you for the lovely phone call. I am reeling from all of it. Hoping to hear from you soon.

She received my letter and photo the same day. Later, she said, "I just got your photo and you know what? When I look at your sweet face, I just know that you're mine."

Those words were like those of a new mother adoring her child and I will always treasure them.

The reunion that was sure to be glorious

A few days later she invited Bob and me to come to her home in Ketchum, Idaho, for a reunion. I got absolutely obsessed over what to wear. I must have bought and exchanged five outfits before finding the right one.

Marian recommended that I take a photo album with photos of myself from birth until the present. I also got neurotic over that! I must have exchanged the photo albums three times. And of course I had to find designer paper to wrap it in—it had to be artistic, like her, so that she would like it…and me. Baby footprints would be the first thing she would see, then a year-by-year chronicle of my life.

Prior to leaving for the reunion, I coached Bob about what he was to do. Poor guy. I wanted *everything* videotaped. I envisioned Bob exiting the plane first and then, when everyone else was off, I would descend the flight of stairs, like Scarlett O'Hara in the movie *Gone with the Wind*, with silk roses in my hands, and run into her waiting arms as we both sobbed with joy.

On the morning of departure, being the good husband that he is, Bob followed my orders.

"Okay," he said, camera rolling and aimed. "Start talking. How are you feeling? Are you ready for this?"

"It is September 5, 1992," I said. "Today I'm going to meet my mother for the very first time. Her name is Marjorie Elizabeth Perry and she lives in a small town in Idaho." I quickly put my fingers over my lip as it began to quiver. "I can't believe I'm so emotional about all of this. Meeting my birth mother is more wonderful than I could have ever imagined."

It seemed like an eternity getting there. I didn't know if I would laugh or cry as the small plane resembling a flying banana approached the tiny airport in the middle of nowhere. No one was in sight when we arrived, save one lonely flight attendant who wheeled a decrepit stairway toward the plane's door. As Bob prepared to deplane, video-cam over his shoulder, I reminded him, "Be sure and get it all on film!"

Goodbye fantasy

The plane emptied quickly. I gathered my belongings while I watched the last person exit. When I was positioning the pink silk roses for Elizabeth over my arm, the attendant peeked into the cabin and said, "Ma'am? You *have* to get off the plane *now*. It's not legal to stay on."

I explained to him that this was a very special occasion and that I had to wait a few minutes before going into the airport. He said he understood, but wouldn't budge. I would have to get off the plane.

So much for my adoptee fantasy of descending the stairs like Scarlett O'Hara in *Gone with the Wind*!

My shaking knees had trouble navigating the narrow portable stairway. As I walked across the tarmac toward the glass entrance door, my body stiffened. It was then that I heard someone cry out, "Oh my God, there she is!"

There she was—the mother I had never met, dressed in cowboy boots and a red suede jacket with fringe on the arms. Quite a contrast to my cream-colored dress pants and sweater. I wondered what I had gotten myself into.

She gave me a quick hug and neither of us laughed or cried. I was numb, or else momentarily regressing. Some professionals say that both birth mothers and adoptees regress to the point of birth when reunited.

Next to her was my half-sister, Debbie, who was not on speaking terms with my mother until she learned of my coming.

"Look at the nose!" Debbie screamed.

I tried to smile.

All the while, Bob was trying to videotape the event. The result was footage of the airport ceiling.

Oops…another adoptee fantasy bites the dust!

We piled into the back of their SUV. Elizabeth, Debbie, and Debbie's husband sat in the front seat and chatted as if Bob and I weren't there. Bob and I rode in silence as he held my hand.

One of Elizabeth's best friends owned an inn and gifted the best suite to Bob and me. The view from the room was beautiful and on the table was a bouquet of purple irises, my favorite flower at that time, with a note that said "From your mother."

When we came to her condo for dinner, she had prepared homemade soup and ordered special bread for the five of us. There was a buffalo head above the fireplace, copper pans hanging from the mantel, and photos of herself on the table next to her easy chair. Nervous laughter punctuated every sentence over dinner.

Conversation then turned to their family memories. At one point my mother went to get a large portrait of herself of when she was younger. I wondered if it had graced the wall of a former home. How I longed to take it home, but didn't have the nerve to ask.

After getting ready for bed that night, I made some notes in my journal:

Today seemed like the longest day. Such a long trip getting here. I felt scared when I met them and somewhat disappointed that they are so different. You can tell Elizabeth is very artistic by the way she dresses and decorates her home. I found out she didn't even know when my birthday was. She truly did forget about me once my birth was over. It became evident as she recounted all the hard things in her life—me being one of them. She has no compassion. It hurts. Deep inside it hurts. I wanted her to say, "I thought about you often." I am disappointed that this is not turning out to be a mountaintop experience, but a painful one. I feel the initial abandonment by her 47 years ago when they all talk and leave Bob and me out. I felt like a stranger. Like I don't belong. I tossed and turned for hours as Bob snored beside me. Finally, I dozed off but woke up again at 6 a.m.

Kept at arm's length

Thanks to social engagements, my mother managed to keep me at arm's length for the first half of the one-week reunion. She kept saying, "This is a happy time for you, but remember it's a painful time for me."

Why would this be such an unhappy time for her? I wondered. *Was I doing something wrong?*

Like many adoptees, I have "antennae" that can sense rejection a mile away. Mine were registering high on the Richter scale.

Bob was only able to stay until midweek because of a business trip. I looked forward to time alone with Elizabeth because we would finally have one-on-one time as mother and daughter. I envisioned us going through the photo album, photo by photo, and me listening to her say how proud she was of me. *Oh, look, you were a cheerleader! You looked beautiful on the homecoming court. Your children are so precious.*

When the time came to give her the photograph album, she opened it, ran her fingers over the tapestry cover, flicked through the pages, and said, "You sure were cute." She then proceeded to close it and push it aside.

The next day one of her wealthy friends gave a luncheon for us. A former movie star came. There was an indoor pool in the basement. Women were dressed to the nines. The diamonds on their hands looked like boulders. Conversation at lunch was about facelifts and tummy tucks.

I sat silently, dressed in my simple black knit dress with roses painted on it.

After lunch one of them asked if we had discovered any similarities. I laughed with delight as I told them that we both love ketchup. No sooner had the words come out of my mouth than Elizabeth approached the group looking at me like she had just sucked the biggest lemon in town.

What was I doing wrong?

That evening as we watched television and chatted, Elizabeth said suddenly, "I've had it up to here," pointing her index finger to her throat in a slitting fashion. "This whole thing is going too fast and too deep for me."

My lip began to quiver and I asked what she meant.

She then reached for the TV remote and turned up the volume several notches.

I told her I was terrified that she was rejecting me and offered to go home early. She said she didn't want me to, reassured me that she would never reject me, and then added that I must be terribly sensitive to have the comments about her stress bother me.

That night, upon returning to the inn, I was desperate. Bob was not within reach and so I called one of Elizabeth's friends who claimed to be an adoption counselor. Just like a wolf in sheep's clothing, she asked me how it was going. I remember saying that Elizabeth didn't have much in her condo, yet her closet was filled with Ralph Lauren bedding. That was not smart!

On the day I left, I asked Elizabeth on the way to the airport if she would like me to take back the photo album. She grabbed the steering wheel, looked straight ahead, and screamed through tears, "You don't know how hard it is to give up a baby! I have thought of you every single day of my life."

"Oh, Elizabeth!" I replied from the back seat. (Her dog was in the front.) "That's the best news I've ever heard! I thought you had forgotten about me."

"Now you're happy that I'm sad," she snapped.

After arriving, I slipped a little gift—an angel figurine that had a verse about mothers attached to it—on the front seat. I knew enough about adoption to realize that for birth mothers saying goodbye is often traumatic, as it triggers that initial separation. I wanted her to be comforted.

While I waited in line to board my plane, she stood alone, looking wistfully through the big airport windows. I imagined that she might be thinking about what life might have been, had she decided to keep me. She came over to me with that same wistful look and said, "I always wanted to be tall like you."

At that moment I looked into her green eyes that were misty with tears and said, "Elizabeth, I love you and am glad you are my mother."

Then I gave her a hug and boarded the plane. My heart was still filled with hope. No, it wasn't a *perfect* reunion, but at least it was a start. We would have years to work on it.

Two days later I called to thank her again for the visit. When I heard the tone of her voice, I felt sick. She began verbally abusing me, taking everything about me and turning it to the most negative interpretation possible. "No more contact," she ordered.

As she was spewing those hurtful words, emphasizing that she wished she would have aborted me, these words came to mind: "Can a mother forget the baby at her breast and have no compassion on the child of her womb? Though she may, I will never forget you."[1]

I ran downstairs to Bob, sobbing. He held me close once again.

Glad to be caught

There's a lot more to my story, which I will share with you later. Perhaps by now you are being caught unaware with thoughts or feelings you didn't know existed. Let me assure you that it is a *good* thing! There are so many advantages to being caught unaware.

"What kind of advantages?" you may be asking. Well, to name a few, the advantage of having an unexpected opportunity to successfully grieve our early-life losses; to enjoy healthy relationships; to develop an unshakable sense of identity; to find our unique purposes in life; and to have peace about our adoption experiences.

I was caught unaware many times in multiple ways during my own healing process, but how glad I am that I was caught. Why? Because now I am alive...fully alive and on the cutting edge of my life's journey. What better place could one be in?

I think you will be pleased to discover that the book you hold in your hands is *for* adoptees, not *about* us! It is a celebration of the fact that we were adopted for a purpose and that adoption is an experience that has the potential of teaching us some of life's richest and deepest lessons.

CHAPTER two

Preparing to Grow

When I first became a grandmother and my twin grandsons were old enough to sit in the little seat on the grocery cart, I took them by the bakery section in the supermarket and asked if they would like a goodie.

I'm sure you know the answer!

They looked wide-eyed at all the sweets and then said, "I want that one."

I'd say, "Okay," and then they would change their minds and choose another item. Two seconds later they'd change their minds again and choose another.

It was very frustrating for this grandma who should have learned the lesson when her own children were young. However, I didn't, and needed to learn it from my wise daughter, Chrissie, who is a fabulous mother.

She said, "Oh, Mom, they don't have the ability to choose yet. It is far too confusing for them—so confusing that they can't make a decision. What you have to do is narrow it down to two goodies. Ask them which of the two they want and then they'll be able to choose."

That's the way it often is for many adoptees. The goodies in the bakery are the choices that we face every day—choices that can lead us to becoming the people we were created to be.

Like my grandsons, however, our ability to choose is often not well-developed. Why? Is there something wrong with us? Far from it! It is because something traumatic happened to us before we ever had words to describe it. The trauma was the loss of our first family, and that had a tremendous impact on our sense of personal power and identity.

As the result of trauma, our foundational belief (often unconscious) is that we don't have the right to choose our own course in life. We believe instead that we are at the mercy of others.

Cheri Freeman is an adoptee activist and owner of Brick Wall Survivors, an online support group for adoptees who have been rejected at reunion. She recalls feeling deprived of choice by the fact that when she was a child, life-altering decisions were made *for* her, to which she was unable to consent but by which she is bound as an adult. She is learning to take back her personal power by making life-transforming choices, but she first had to face the fact that losing her sense of personal power at such a profound level early in life impaired her ability to choose some of the life-giving options available.

Like Cheri, and like my young grandsons in the bakery, we might be right in front of the goodies (choices), but they don't seem "choosable" to us. They are a blur. The result? We see ourselves as victims and don't have the confidence to choose.

The "V" word

Some of you may be saying, "No way! I never have nor will I ever fall into the category you are describing. I am successful in every area of life."

I hear you. I also believed I had my act together, as did almost everyone else in my world. I thought I was making good choices and was in control of my life. But when my adoption door began to creak open at midlife, I started to discover that a victim mindset can be hidden beneath a variety of lifestyles, including successful ones, depending on our personalities and our resilience.

Certainly, not *all* adoptees feel or act like victims—just as not all the topics discussed in this book apply to all adoptees. Not all adoptees were newborns. Some were traumatized by abusive parents and taken away by child protective services. Some languished in orphanages. Some were adopted internationally and have no birth history whatsoever.

If you don't immediately identify with the word "victim," I'd encourage you to set aside any preconceived ideas about where you are in regard to this subject. Shift into neutral gear for just a few minutes and hear what the experts—our fellow adoptees— have to say about this topic.

First, what do I mean by "victim"? Well, *The Synonym Finder* spells it out pretty well: "sufferer, injured one, dupe, sucker, sap, poor fish, chump, schnook, winner of the booby prize, easy or soft mark, sitting duck, patsy, fall guy, soft touch, pushover, laughing stock, butt, fair game, and everybody's fool."[1]

I sometimes hear adoptees and professionals say in a droning tone of voice, "Adoption is a lifelong journey." They make it sound like we have to walk around for the rest of our lives with balls and chains around our ankles because of early-life trauma.

I don't believe this!

Because adoption is a lifelong journey, we have a future filled with the potential to learn invaluable lessons. But many of us *haven't been taught* that we have a *choice* in every situation in life.

This was the case with 66-year-old Connie Dawson, Ph.D., an educator in the fields of parenting and adoption, and co-author of *Growing Up Again: Parenting Ourselves, Parenting Our Children* and also *How Much Is Enough?* She says that she's only consciously recognized herself as a victim since becoming aware about how her first experiences in life affected her earliest, and subsequent, decisions about others and herself.

Adoptee Frieda Moore, an adoption support group leader and lay counselor, says that it wasn't until her mid-thirties that she realized she had many options in life. Because profound and permanent decisions were made for her at birth, and no one taught her she had choices about how to respond, she lived according to her natural inclination, which was to always let others make choices for her.

What is the result of being a victim and letting others control us? Resentment toward those we think are withholding freedom. Author Judith Viorst says, "Some of us, in fact, will passively settle for a state of genetic victimhood, willing to define ourselves as helpless playthings of forces beyond our control."[2]

But does it always have to be this way? Do we have to remain victims for the rest of our lives? No! We *can* choose! We *can* learn how to make choices from all the goodies in the bakery. We *can* live with a deep sense of personal power, freedom, and identity.

Let's begin by looking at how a victim's mindset is created and take a closer look at a portrait of a victim.

How the victim mentality begins

Authors Rosamund and Benjamin Zander give us a good start at understanding the origin of "victim thinking." They say,

Experiments in neuroscience have demonstrated that we reach an understanding of the world in roughly this sequence: first, our senses bring us selective information about what is out there; second, the brain constructs its own simulation of sensations; and only then, third, do we have our first conscious experience of our milieu. The world comes into our consciousness in the form of a map already drawn, a story already told, a hypothesis, a construction of our own making.[3]

Let's apply the Zanders' theory to our situations as adoptees. First, after birth our senses brought selective information about what was "out there." More often than not, that information was a primal sense of "She's gone. I am all alone." Second, our brains constructed simulations of sensations—sensations of abject terror and panic, I would guess. Third, we had our first conscious experience of the world, which, for many adoptees separated at birth from their birth mothers, is inevitably, "This world is not a safe place. I am helpless." Older adoptees who have been removed from their homes because of neglect or abuse are likely to deduce the same negative messages.

Thus, many of us, either at birth or as children or teens, developed the core belief that other people and circumstances control our lives, and we have lived accordingly.

How does this flesh out in everyday life? How can we tell if we are thinking and behaving like victims?

A portrait of a victim

A victim is someone who believes he is at the mercy of everything and everybody. But more important, a victim is at the mercy of his own personal thoughts, feelings, and beliefs. There is little feeling of control; instead, the primary feelings are of *being* controlled. Victims see themselves as powerless. They believe they have limited choices in life. They sabotage themselves even when others believe in them. If I were to sum up the victim mentality in two words, I would say *no control*.

And what do victims want more than anything?

'Control! Or, more precisely, *freedom* from the control of others. Freedom of choice. Freedom to choose what is best. Freedom to draw boundaries with others and not feel guilty. Freedom to be true to their own growth process and cheerfully dismiss the insensitive remarks of others. Freedom to dream and envision what wonderful things might lie ahead.

However, taking a look at the following characteristics of a victim, we see that the opposite is true.

Frustrated and confused

Many fellow adoptees could identify with my grandsons' confusion with making choices. Dr. Richard Gilbert, BCC, D. Min., is the director of the World Pastoral Care Center and author of *Finding Your Way After Your Parent Dies: Hope for Adults*. He says, "Age has only added to the frustration. As I get older, the questions about adoption seem to be more complex and perplexing."

Shirley A. Reynolds, a freelance writer, outreach volunteer, and employee of the Federal Probation Department, says that she felt confused as a child in elementary school when someone would say, "It must be awful to not know who your *real* parents are!"

Trish DePew, age thirty, wife, mother of two preschoolers, and co-leader of an adoption support group, says, "I get confused about enforcing my boundaries and then I feel angry because people are taking advantage of me."

Another aspect of the victim mindset is powerlessness.

Powerless and at the mercy of others

What do you picture when you read "powerless" and "at the mercy of others"? For me, I remember when one of my counselors asked me to visit a local hospital nursery to try and discover what I had lost when my birth mother disappeared from my life at birth.

A nurse friend and I gowned up and went to the nursery she worked in. What impressed me was the innocence and dependence of those babies who were going to be adopted. They were clearly *at the mercy* of circumstance and people. Later that day I penned these words:

Oh little baby, so soft and pure. How sweet and precious you are. How could anyone give you away? How could anyone act like you don't exist? There you are—so tiny and helpless, lying there in that incubator. Isolated and cut off from all human touch. Not a sound around you. Only a bottle to feed you. No nurturing, warm breast. No mother's arms. No one. There is no one for you. Oh, little baby. I feel so sorry for you. How could anyone forget about you? You are so very precious. You are so beautiful. No one to protect you. No one to care for you. No one to sing lullabies to you. No one. You have no idea of the struggles you will go through in the years ahead because of this. You have no idea that you will be terrified of abandonment and rejection and that you will prefer isolation to people. You just sleep on, as if there is not a care for you in the world. You have no idea that volcanic anger has been born in your breast toward the one who gave you away. You have no idea that the seeds of fear lay buried in your heart, ready to ripen as the years go by. You have no idea what unconditional love and abiding mean. You have no idea. You just sleep on.

Kasey Hamner, a school psychologist in California, licensed educational psychologist, and author of *Whose Child? An Adoptee's Healing Journey from Relinquishment to Reunion and Beyond* and *Adoption Forum*, says that she feels like a victim of circumstance. The adoption agency failed her in many ways, by not thoroughly investigating her adoptive home, and by not doing follow-up through the years. "That is a huge problem with the system," Kasey says. "They place babies and assume that everything will run smoothly. In my case, that was *wrong*!"

Plagued by self-pity

Self-pity is an insidious parasite that sucks the life out of us, like an octopus with its prey. When we allow others to take away our power of choice, we feel trapped, and it's easy to feel sorry for ourselves. We often throw a party and invite the three proverbial guests: me, myself, and I!

Kimberly Steiner, a twenty-seven-year-old Korean adoptee who is dealing with cultural as well as adoption issues, has moved from a sense of abandonment to acceptance. She says that when she's dealing with adoption feelings and issues, she secretly thinks like a victim and does the "poor me" thing.

Even though we may be having a pity party inside, we often put on a strong façade.

Hidden behind a strong façade

This is one of the "acceptable" ways we can unknowingly become and remain a victim. We are not off in the corner having a pity party. Heavens…that's the last thing we would ever do. We present a strong façade instead. We are the perfectionists of the world. The overachievers. The outwardly successful.

But what is the motivation behind all of this seeming success?

A counselor friend once told of an adolescent female who came into her office acting as tough as could be. Her parents had done everything to keep her from acting out in destructive ways. When my friend asked, "So, how long have you been too much to handle?" the girl's perfect mask crumbled, revealing a young woman who felt like a victim and who was in incredible emotional pain.

Here is a poem I wrote some time ago about my former (most of the time) strong façade:

An Ode to Insecurity
Please, don't let my strength fool you,
*   For it's only a veneer you see*
Built up from years of silence
*   From those who I would their victim be.*
I need for you to see the person deep down inside,
*   Who beneath the veneer is trying to hide.*
For years I didn't know it was adoption,
*   Then I got depressed and believed I had no options.*
But now I am beginning to see
*   All the people who have victimized me.*
I feel frustrated, ashamed, and abandoned.
*   Is there any way out?*
Will I ever be free?
*   Please deliver me.*
Where can I go?
*   Where can I flee?*
Will anyone ever believe me?
*   When people look at my perfect life*
They think it is absent of shame and strife.
*   But it's only an illusion, filled with delusion*
A life of desperate seclusion.
*   Where can I go?*
Where can I flee?
*   Who will let me just be me?*

Pretty pathetic, huh?

Richard Curtis, cofounder of the Adoption Triad of the Treasure Coast support group serving St. Lucie and Martin counties in Florida, says he became the "silent son." He learned quickly that keeping silent and asking no questions was the safest path to choose.

Connie Dawson says:

> For years, I didn't think I could afford to have an experience of being adopted, for if I did *and* talked about it, I risked being shunned; the usual family messages were to "stop right there." Shunning is dangerous and leaves the one being shunned alone and feeling unsafe in a primal way. Once one has experienced the ultimate shunning of being sent away in early life, into the frightening and inhospitable desert, so to speak, deep-bone knowledge reminds one to be careful, for being abandoned again is always an option.

Saboteur of relationships

So how does the victim feel about himself? Does he feel that he is worthy of success, acceptance, and well-being? Far from it. The victim mindset says: "I am a loser. I am worthy only of rejection. Therefore I will set the stage for it and make it happen before others have an opportunity to reject and hurt me."

Todd, age twenty-nine, does this in his relationships with women. He says that he tests them to see if they will leave him by seeing how much they will take of his passive-aggressive behavior. But here's the clincher. He says, "The end result is always the same…it feels like I am unworthy and being rejected, but in actuality I give them no choice but to leave."

Beverly says that she also tests people to see if they *really* like her. But she says that they always fail, which is her sad little proof that she can't be loved. She builds up resentments about the failures of the people she loves, and distances herself from them.

"Instead of waiting to be rejected, I will most likely do something outrageous so that the other person will reject me," admits Kimberly Steiner.

Liberation

The aforementioned characteristics aren't an exhaustive list of a victim's mentality and behavior, but they give us a launching pad to begin assessing if we fall into the victim category. If we *do* identify, what is the answer? What can we do to get rid of this victim thinking that has plagued some of us since birth? How can we find liberation—the longed-for freedom to make our own life-giving choices?

First, many of us need help in acknowledging our reality. Joe Soll, CSW, author of *Adoption Healing: A Path to Recovery* and creator of the Annual March on Washington for Civil Rights and Healing Weekends, says:

> I felt like a victim until I began to understand that losing my mother at the beginning of my life hampered my ability to have good, intimate friendships, and experience my emotions. I think all of us adoptees, *and* our mothers, were victims and remain that way until we find a way to get some help in dealing with our issues. Then we can easily remove our victim status.

And how do we get this kind of help? Probably the best way is by listening to the stories of other adoptees, getting professional counseling, joining an all-adoptee support group, and talking in-depth with a fellow adoptee. But *self-intervention* is possible as well, according to Spencer Johnson, MD. One of his clients said:

> Sometimes I start feeling like I'm not getting a fair shake. Usually it's over something small. I still don't like it very much when I feel I'm not being treated well. But as soon as I stop and see that I'm feeling like a victim, I know who my persecutor is. Myself. Soon I remember that I can either be my best friend or my worst enemy. It all depends on what I choose to think and choose to do.[4]

I chose self-intervention for my victim thinking when the late beloved adoption author and speaker, Betty Jean Lifton, encouraged participants at an American Adoption Congress (AAC) to write a letter to the victim part within us. Here's what I wrote:

Dear victim part of me,

I've used you long enough. You no longer have to be loyal to those who hurt you. You can speak up. You can say it like it is. You no longer have to be the good girl. I empower you to grow to maturity. No longer give people power over you. Others have nothing more than you do. Don't let them take your power away. Don't let them tell you what to do. Tell them how you feel when they play God in your life and tell you what to do. I'm on a healing journey and because of that I feel less like a victim.

Right now you may be distressed by the reality of what your mind has been thinking all these years and may feel further victimized. That's okay. Often, we need to be overwhelmed before we're ready to grow.

Our new goal is an unshakable identity

Before we launch into our twenty truths and corresponding choices, let's begin to refocus, even if it is ever so slowly. We need to look in a new direction as we make the choices, and some of us have never seen that option. We've been stuck in reverse!

The new direction is "up." We must learn to see ourselves not as victims of trauma, not how others treat us, not how we've blown it in the past. Instead, we need to begin looking at ourselves in new, positive ways.

I love this poem. It has certainly inspired me, and perhaps may inspire you to begin letting go of your past and to look not only *up* but also *forward* to the wonderful future ahead of you:

A single thread in a tapestry,
Though its color brightly shine,
Can never see its purpose
In the pattern of the grand design…
So how can you see what your life is worth,
Or where your value lies?
You can never see through the eyes of man,
You must look at your life—
Look at your life through heaven's eyes. [5]

As we make our choices with an upward and forward focus, we won't even know ourselves a few years from now! We will be people with an unshakable identity, whose lives just happened to have been touched by adoption. I am honored to be on this life-transforming journey with you!

The following chapters will present you with a truth and then with a choice, which, if appropriated, will prove life-transforming.

part TWO

Twenty Truths and Twenty Choices That Can Transform

The remarkable thing we have is a choice every day regarding the attitude we will embrace for that day. We cannot change our past… We cannot change the fact that people will act in a certain way. We cannot change the inevitable. The only thing we can do is play on the one string we have, and that is our attitude.

—CHARLES SWINDOLL

Instead of looking at life as a narrowing funnel, we can see it ever widening to choose the things we want to do, to take the wisdom we've learned and create something.

—LIZ CARPENTER

Mother is the name for God in the lips and hearts of little children.

—WILLIAM M. THACKERAY

three

Thoughts about Our Birth Parents Are Innate

I have yet to meet an adoptee who can honestly claim to have never thought about his or her birth mother, especially on birthdays.

It's no wonder. Just think about how intimately we were united with the woman who gave us birth! What a connection we had for at least nine months. An inseparable bond. As inseparable as tea from hot water. As inseparable as a bud from the stem of a flower. As inseparable as the ocean from the sand.

Renowned author John Bowlby says that the mother is the hub of life.[1]

Author and physician Peter Nathananielsz says that much of the way our bodies work is molded and solidified during our time in the womb, and that there are critical periods during prenatal development when our cells and organs decide how they will behave for the rest of our lives.[2] Just think…at the very moment of conception, our entire genetic code was established that determined our sex and the color of our hair and eyes. At three weeks we had a beating heart, and at forty days detectable brain waves.

Perhaps even more fascinating is a phenomenon that goes on between a mother and her unborn child that absolutely boggled my mind when I learned about it…

Our first conversations with her

Who do you think was the first person with whom you had a conversation?

Would you believe it was your birth mother?

And, where and when do you think it might have happened?

This is the mind-boggling part—in the womb!

Dr. Thomas Verny says that during the last three months of pregnancy, and especially the last two, we are mature enough physically and intellectually to send and receive fairly sophisticated messages to and from our mothers. Our mothers set the pace, provide the cues, and actually mold our responses.[3]

What messages did we get from our birth mothers? I believe it all depended on their attitudes toward us. If we heard, "I love you and am so glad you're a part of me. I will do all that I can to help you develop into the person you were created to be. I can't wait to see you. I will welcome you into the world in a way more wonderful than you can possibly imagine," our response would certainly have been positive. We would have thrived on it. "Oh, Mommy," our little pre-verbal minds might have "said," "I love you so much and I can't wait to be born so that I can nurse at your breasts and be held in your arms."

On the other hand, what if we heard, "I don't want you. I don't even like you. In fact, I think of you as an 'it,' and frankly, I can't wait to get rid of you. I wish I could"?

Our little minds may have responded like this: "All alone. All alone. Hurts so bad. No one will ever take care of me. I must 'buck up' and be strong so I can survive. Be strong. Be strong. Tense up. Be on guard so I won't be tortured like this again."

This kind of message to us would be unimaginably painful. Author Judith Viorst likens it to being doused with oil and set on fire.[4]

But it's a subconscious pain. Dr. Arthur Janov says that this kind of pain is:

> Not like a pinch where we yell 'ouch,' shake our fingers, and in a few minutes get over it. Instead, it's like being pinched so hard you cannot feel it, so that the pain goes on forever because it is continually being processed below the level of conscious awareness. It doesn't mean it is not there doing its damage—it just means that it is too much to feel.[5]

Some of us can identify with those negative conversations, and many of them are still playing in our heads even though they were communicated so many years ago. Some of us feel at a cellular level that we *need* our mothers' love and welcoming attitude in order to survive. If we experienced a transracial adoption, this may escalate as we hit the teen years. Every time we look in the mirror, we wonder who we look like.

Who did my skin color come from?

I know for a fact that I didn't have my birth mother's love from day one, yet by grace, I am a survivor. As my husband always says, "From some people you learn *what* to do and from others you learn what *not* to do."

Whatever the case, whether conversations with our birth mothers were positive or painful, prenatal experiences are encoded in our bodies, souls, and spirits, resulting in questions and thoughts that pop into our minds, often unexpectedly, throughout our lives.

Our first thoughts about her

Folks who aren't adopted are often amazed at how early some of us think about our birth mothers, especially when I tell the story about the adopted girl who asked her mom prior to her third birthday party if her "lady" was coming. The mother asked what lady she was talking about. Her daughter answered, "The lady I grew inside. It's my *birthday*, isn't it?"[6]

Cheri Freeman also thought about her origins at an early age. She told herself stories at age three or four about how her birth parents missed her and how happy they would be to finally meet her.

Joe Soll says that from the moment he knew he was adopted at age four, there has never been a day that he hasn't thought about his birth mom.

Frieda Moore found comfort when hurting by imagining her birth mother coming to find and rescue her, taking her home to live with her forever.

Pam Hasegawa, a fifty-nine-year-old adoptee advocate, says that when she had the lead in a play, she remembers thinking, "If she could only see me now! Would she be proud of me?"

Where did those positive attitudes come from? Could they have begun in the womb?

And what about those of us who have negative attitudes? Laurie, even as a young child, worried that her birth mother must be struggling and depressed. Others of us didn't begin to think about our birth mothers until we hit puberty and shot up to six feet tall, even though both our adoptive parents were short. Shirley Reynolds says that when she became a teen, she realized that she looked very different to her adoptive family. This propelled her into a fantasy world where her mother would be dark-haired and petite, like Shirley. And, of course, she would be beautiful!

If we are of mixed race, we look at our skin color and wonder what race our birth mother is. Is she Indian or African-American?

Some adoptees claim to never think about their birth mothers. Sally says that she feels guilty because she doesn't think about hers, knowing that so many other adoptees do.

Sally is not alone. Many don't think about their birth mothers for various reasons, but the reason may possibly be shame. Shame is that awful feeling, not that we have *done* something wrong, but that something is inherently wrong with *us* as a person. In adoptee language, "My life is a mistake."

How about hearing your adoptive mother talk derogatively about the twenty-one-year-old down the street who was unmarried and pregnant, raving about how much shame she brought to her family? Connie Dawson heard this message at the tender age of ten as her mother delivered a veiled message that Connie herself was shameful and shouldn't be "bad," like her birth mother was. Or how about Sue who struggles with a haunting belief that something dreadful must lurk within her, which, if found out by her adoptive parents, would cause them to bolt from her?

Or how about being a black child with white parents and hearing others ask why your parents adopted a black child? How about when you're only six years old and people come up to your mom at the grocery store and ask how she fixes your Afro-American hair? Or, if you're a black teen and you walk into a convenience store with your white parent, you don't experience "white privilege" even though your mom is white. Others look suspiciously at you instead.

Her lifelong impact

Whether positive or negative, and whether we like it or not, our birth mothers are a "forever" part of us. How we choose to respond to that reality will deeply influence the course of our lives.

Author Louise Kaplan says that in the death of a parent (which I believe can be likened to relinquishment), the dialogue between parent and child continues within, the child and the child remains attached in profound ways to that dialogue throughout life.[7]

When my dad died, one of his friends said to me, "You never lose your parents. They are always a part of you." In my grief, I was rather skeptical, but since that time I have found it to be true. For instance, after every meal, Dad, in a mischievous way, picked up the unused silverware saying, "This one's clean!" We'd all laugh and say, "Yeah, Dad!" Over the years it became an endearing behavior, and in the years since his death, whenever I pick up clean silverware after a meal, I think of him and smile.

What about our birth fathers?

We have examined a very important part of our existence—our birth mothers. But what about our birth *fathers*? Did they have no influence? Last time I checked the books on reproduction, it takes two to make a baby.

When I was almost finished with the final draft of this book I talked with a reunited birth father who adored his daughter but who had been rejected by her. His heart was breaking as he wept while telling me that he would do anything to have a meaningful father–daughter relationship.

Do many birth fathers feel the same way? Would they want a relationship with us if they had the opportunity? Do they feel the loss of us to the same degree that birth mothers usually do? As we do?

What if our birth fathers are rapists or serial murderers? Many of us were conceived in rape. How are we to tell our stories? How are we to believe our lives are not a mistake?

As I've said, I believe that adoption can be likened to a big door. Over the top of the door is written "Birth Mother," for our thoughts about her usually come first. It is often *after* we have gone through the adoption door that we find the words "Birth Father" written on the other side.

Ron Hilliard, of Palm Beach Heights, Florida, focused mainly on his birth mother and blocked out thoughts of his birth father because his father didn't want to marry his mother and had also urged her to have an abortion. Ron's search for his birth mother ended in a cemetery, and he is now looking at the back of the adoption door and wondering who his father is—and who he is as a result. This curiosity is being fueled by the fact that Ron has a fraternal twin brother who resembles his birth mother's photos, while Ron doesn't. This makes him wonder who he *does* resemble.

Some of us see the words "Birth Father" first on the adoption door. Richard Curtis says that the loss of his birth father was the first loss of a male figure in his life, followed by the loss of his adoptive father when he was only five years old. As a result, Richard had no male role models and was left with what he terms a "father hunger" that he believes many adoptees experience.

Like Ron, Richard's search for his birth father ended at a tombstone. However, after finding people who knew his father prior to his death, Richard can see that many of the choices and behaviors he has made in his life closely parallel his birth father's.

Crystal speaks of father hunger by calling it a "void" that colors her relationships with men, and keeps her longing for a father even though she is forty years old. A friend recently asked her what she would do if she ever found him. To Crystal the answer was simple—"I'd quit my job, move in with him, and have him take care of me." She then added, "I am joking… but not really."

When our curiosity is aroused, our speculations about our birth father increase. What kind of a person was/is he? Did he refuse any responsibility and abandon our birth mother, as in Laurie's case? Out of deep hurt, she says she prejudged him as a jerk because he chose not to marry her mom or encourage her to keep her baby. She is actually happy that she doesn't have to know him.

To Issie, her birth father is a non-issue. A few years ago she thought briefly about trying to locate him, but her fear of rejection was too strong. In addition, she has no proof, short of DNA, of who her father is.

Then there's the nasty subject of incest. Sheila says that her birth father is her mother's stepdad. She's glad he died before she met her birth family because she doesn't know how she would react to him. She's accepted that he's a part of her, yet she can't comprehend his deplorable actions.

Dawn Saphir, twenty-seven, born in Seoul, Korea, and adopted at six months of age by a Caucasian family, says that based on what she's learned of Korean culture at the time of her birth, she doesn't have a lot of positive feelings about who her birth father may have been.

Some of our birth fathers may be completely ignorant of the fact that we even exist.

How might our lives have been different had they been informed?

Karen Stinger says that she feels a great tenderness for the father who never knew about her. "He never had the chance to 'give me up,'" she explains. "He never had the chance to know he was a father."

Renee Mills says that she recently had the amazing experience of finding her birth father, and that the hardest part was discovering that he never even knew her birth mother was pregnant.

As I finish this section, I am reminded of my own birth father. Even as I write, he doesn't seem real, for I have never met him, nor do I have any hope of meeting him because my birth mother refuses to reveal his identity. I know, however, that he is a forever part of me because I am always searching for him, even on a subconscious level. For me, this searching didn't really begin until after I met my birth mother.

The only things my birth mother told me about my father were that he was "a very nice man" and that he was tall and had red hair. I never knew where my oldest daughter, Lisa, got her beautiful red hair, but now I do. When I look at her, I often wonder about him. Not long ago I sat next to an attractive elderly gentleman on a plane. Guess what my first thought was? *I wonder if he could be my birth dad.*

I had a dad in the growing-up years who loved me dearly and whom I loved. But I also have *another* dad out there somewhere who may not even know I exist. I would like to know about him, but at this point don't believe I want to meet him. My sugar-coating attitude has dissipated over the years. He had raped my birth mother. Case closed.

Our dual identity

If we were created from the very fiber of our birth parents' physical and emotional beings, don't you think our need to think about them would be innate? If we had in-utero conversations with our mother in the womb, wouldn't you say it is natural for us to think about her as we are growing up and growing old? And if our birth father's DNA helped determine the color of our hair and eyes, wouldn't you say that he is just as much a part of us as our mother?

Wherever we are in the spectrum of perceptions about our birth parents, we must rest assured that our thoughts are normal. They are part of the fiber of our being. Part of the package of being adopted. It's all about our identity...our dual identity. Most of all, it's about establishing an unshakable identity by integrating all the parts of who we are—body, soul, and spirit.

So what must we do for ourselves? What healthy choice must we make to move closer toward an unshakable identity?

Our Choice

To give ourselves permission to think about and discuss openly our birth parents, especially with our adoptive parents.

Giving ourselves permission to let natural thoughts surface reminds me of when I am getting sick. I feel nausea and the urge to be sick to my stomach. I hate that more than anything, so I concentrate on something else so that I won't. But when I finally let myself think about the possibility, up comes my lunch, followed by an incredible feeling of relief. A similar sensation often results when we allow ourselves to freely think about our birth parents. The urge to do so is really unstoppable.

Penny Callan Partridge, beloved poet of the adoption world who has been active in the adoption reform community since 1973, writes:

Pandora in Later Life

And what if I had not?
I would be dead by now.
Dead of my anger.
Dead of my goodness.
Dead of my anger
at my stinking goodness.
Imagine yourself
in a room with a box.
And you don't know
what's in it.
And you don't know
why you shouldn't.
When you closed your eyes,
you would see that box.
When you opened your eyes,
you would see that box.
That box was my life.
My life was in the box.
When I opened the box,
I was letting out my life.
Oh you get blamed
because of other people's
closed boxes. But even
with all of the openings
and closings my life
has been since then,
I have
not
ever
once
even
a single
second
regretted it.[8]

Perhaps all these thoughts are new to you. You want to begin your process of making positive, life-transforming choices but don't know how. The following section will help. (You'll find such a section at the end of every chapter.)

How to begin

- *Try free-association writing.* Write whatever comes to mind about your birth parents. No one is ever going to see it, so be as free as possible. When you are done, look back and discern basic themes that run throughout your piece.

- *Make a drawing.* Imagine "the adoption door," and draw both the front and back sides. Label whose title is over the doorpost—birth mother or birth father. Then ask yourself, "Where am I in this scene? Am I a casual observer, am I moving closer toward it, or am I knocking on the door?" Then draw yourself in the picture.

- *Write a letter TO and FROM your birth mother and father.* Experts say that this is one of the most effective tools for adoptees to get in touch with buried thoughts and feelings. Pay attention to your body language as you write. Find a trusted friend and read your letters out loud to him or her. Be aware of your emotions as you read and record them later at the bottom of the letters. Be sure to date them too!

- If you are in an open adoption, write a piece about what you think it might have been like to be parented by your birth parents. What struggles do you think may have been added to your journey?

- If your adoption was transracial and transcultural, can you identify specific questions or confusions about your parentage?

Now that we've given ourselves permission to let thoughts about our birth parents rise to the surface, we may begin to have painful, mixed feelings about our adoption experiences. We'll discuss that next.

Like both sides of a coin, the emotions present seem to be opposite, yet they both exist side by side.

—RON HILLIARD

CHAPTER four

Painful Thoughts about Our Adoptions Are Normal

Have you ever run your fingernails over a blackboard? I have, and my gut reaction is to cringe, curl up my fingers, and wince until the physical and aural discomfort I've just experienced has passed.

Did you know that there is a similar finger-over-the-blackboard *psychological* sensation that occurs when incoming information doesn't line up with our built-in belief systems? Clinicians call it "cognitive dissonance," but lay people like us simply call it "mixed feelings." Lately, I've wondered if "mixed feelings" is psychobabble for "painful feelings." I like to call it like it is, don't you? It's important that we understand this psychological phenomenon because it has a strong impact on our lives...for most of us, anyway.

Where do painful feelings originate?

Every baby born into this world innately expects that his or her mother will provide connection, nurture, and love. That's the way we're wired in the womb, adopted or not. However, that privilege of being cared for by the one who gave us birth didn't occur for many of us who were adopted. It might have occurred for a short time before we were relinquished, but eventually the painful separation came.

We expected and needed to drink from her breasts, lie on her warm body, and hear the sound of her familiar voice. But instead we were placed into the arms of strangers. Loving strangers, in most cases; nevertheless, they *were* strangers to us at the time.

This experience frequently produces mixed sensory feelings. Incoming information—"I am being held by someone that doesn't sound, smell, or look like my mommy"—doesn't line up with "I love the feel, sound, and smell of my mommy. In her arms I feel so safe."

Our basic belief system is being violated. Maybe that's why many of us often feel an unexplainable sense of chaos and anxiety, like something inside just isn't right.

Cheri Freeman knows that adoption brings joy to many people, and even to her. Yet she has a deep sadness that she is trying to overcome, stemming from the fact that a mother who gives you life is supposed to *love* you and *keep* you, not discard you.

Adoptive parents often say about adoption day: "It was the happiest day of our lives!" While most adoptees are happy to be adopted, our memories tell us that adoption day was the most painful day of our lives, as the person with whom we shared deep intimacy suddenly disappeared from our world.

Ron Hilliard says that almost everyone showered him with the positive aspects of being adopted. "You are loved," they would say. Yet in his heart he didn't *experience* being loved. "I felt unloved, given away, and unwanted," he says.

Frieda Moore says she "felt like an intruder—unloved, unwanted, and not worth loving," even though her parents lavished her with unconditional love.

Shefalie Chandra had mixed feelings due to a mixed heritage. Her skin tone caused much confusion and a deep sadness within her, even when she was later placed in foster care.

I am confident that Moses, an adoptee who lived more than 2000 years ago, experienced similar mixed feelings. He was born to an Israelite family, who, along with the rest of the Israelite nation, was in slavery under the wicked Pharaoh of Egypt.

The more the Israelites multiplied, the meaner the Pharaoh became. Finally he sent an edict throughout the Israelite huts that all male babies must be killed at birth by the midwives.

Just imagine how Jochebed and Amram, Moses' parents, felt when Jochebed was pregnant during this time. Of course you couldn't learn the sex of a baby during those times, but I can just see Jochebed fearing the worst when she heard the Pharaoh's soldiers riding through the village, shouting the death edict.

Jochebed delivered a boy, but the midwives valued life and didn't kill him or other male babies at their births. This sent the Pharaoh into a rage and he gave a second edict: all male babies must be drowned in the River Nile at birth.

Jochebed probably kept the curtains on her windows shut so that the soldiers riding by couldn't see her baby. I can imagine her holding Moses close in fear that a loud cry would bring a fast death. They didn't have pacifiers then, but if he didn't need nursing, perhaps she put the tip of her little finger in his mouth for him to suck on. Anything to keep him quiet.

One day when Jochebed was nursing, an idea came. She would make a watertight basket coated with tar and pitch that was just big enough to hold her son. There would be a lid that would cover him and protect him from the sun and insects.

She knew that the Pharaoh's daughter Hatshepsut came to the Nile to bathe daily. Jochebed believed that Hatshepsut would hear Moses' cry or see him in the basket and have pity on him and let him live.

Jochebed rehearsed this plan with her daughter, Miriam, as she was going to be a key player in the plan to save the baby. "You hide behind a tree, and when the Pharaoh's daughter discovers and opens the basket, she will look for a wet nurse. That's when you are to approach her and say that you know of someone who would be willing."

Jochebed was able to keep the baby's cries muffled for a few weeks. But when the cries got louder, she knew it was time to implement her plan. As she carried her beloved son down to the Nile, hot tears streamed down her cheeks as she softly sang him his last lullaby.

When she let go of the basket, she quickly hid behind some brush. The baby sent out heart-wrenching wails and every scream felt like a knife to the heart. Every time she heard a cry, her breasts engorged with milk, which reminded her in a vivid way of the separation from her baby. She buried her face in her hands, sobbing.

I have often wondered how Moses reacted emotionally to being in a dark, stuffy basket. A totally foreign place. A place where all human connections were broken. The record simply says, "He was crying."[1] The root of that word means "to weep, bewail, mourn, sob, weep continually, weep longer, wept bitterly."[2]

Jochebed's plan for her baby was carried out to the last detail. She was asked to be the wet nurse for Hatshepsut until the time of weaning, which, during those times, was about four years of age. Thus, in an incredible turn of events, Jochebed once again held the child she cherished. It seemed overwhelming to grasp the fact that the daughter of the one who wanted her baby annihilated was the one who snatched him from the jaws of death. I can imagine Moses' mother recounting how he was miraculously saved and returned, but don't you wonder if every time he heard the story, he may have experienced unexplainable anxiety?

The years flew by quickly until it was time for Moses to be weaned. Before they knew it, the dreaded day had arrived. Can't you imagine Jochebed and Amram on the evening before the adoption? She may have gathered his favorite toys and clothes and put them in a sack while Amram may have been in the other room, silently rehearsing a child-friendly explanation of the upcoming adoption. All the while he was praying. *Where should I begin? How can a four-year-old child possibly understand that we are going to stop being his parents and give him to someone else?*

When the grieving family walked together to the Pharaoh's palace, Hatshepsut, the adoptive mother, was eagerly awaiting their arrival. Moses clung to Jochebed as they approached the palace. A servant dressed in Egyptian finery opened the huge brass doors and ushered them in. What a contrast the shiny marble floors, tall pillars, and statues of Egyptian gods were to Moses' simple family abode.

In flowing silk robes and a high hat covered with jewels, Hatshepsut greeted them with outstretched arms. "I am so glad to see you, son! I thought this day would never arrive."

After a few minutes of awkward pleasantries, Amram, Jochebed, Miriam, and Aaron, Moses' birth brother, said, "We have to go now, Moses. You will be staying here from now on. We love you and will never forget you."

As Jochebed handed her son over to Hatshepsut, he screamed, "Mama, Papa, don't go!" They gave him one last emotional embrace, turned their backs, and walked out. His body stiffened as he pushed Hatshepsut away.

Even though Jochebed and Amram's hearts were breaking, they sacrificially let go of their son, knowing that there was a higher purpose for him. A specific role in human history.

And that turned out to be true. Moses became one of the greatest leaders of all time. That gives us hope as adoptees!

But Moses was in a place of raw loss. All that was familiar was suddenly gone.

Can't you imagine his adoptive mother reminding him as he grew up of the joyous day he walked through the palace doors? I don't know about you, but I think Moses would have had painful feelings, big time.

How to recognize painful adoption-related feelings

Attachment and bonding specialist Gregory C. Keck, Ph.D., says:

> The concept of cognitive dissonance is a tough one even for adult adoptees to understand, and even if they understand it, I don't think that the understanding mitigates the feelings of abandonment. Actually, I'm not sure there is any explanation or reason that adoptees can embrace to resolve their loss. That's not to say that people don't get through it. Obviously, they do.[3]

Dr. Keck makes it clear that cognitive dissonance is one of the highest hurdles adoptees must jump. Therefore, our first order of business will be to identify two common markers that may indicate mixed feelings—something that produces a finger-over-the-blackboard sensation psychologically. One is hypervigilance, and the other is anxiety.

Hypervigilance

The Synonym Finder says this about vigilance: "watchfulness, guardedness, wariness, caution, forethought, keenness, sleeplessness."[4]

Magnify those words by 100 percent and we have hypervigilance!

Sometimes hypervigilance comes in handy, for example, if a car is crossing the median and heading directly toward us. Or when a toddler has fallen into the deep end of a pool. We can be "Johnny on the spot," which can be good. But at other times, it's distressing. Our systems are constantly working overtime to sort out dissonant beliefs and emotions.

Therapist and best-selling author and speaker Nancy Verrier says:

> Although the adoptee might not be consciously aware of the fear of abandonment, which is then felt as free-floating anxiety, there is an attitude which can be readily discerned. It is a kind of watchfulness or cautious testing of the environment, which is called hypervigilance.[5]

Lois Rabey, an author and speaker who was adopted at nine days of age, says that one of the ways hypervigilance manifests itself in her life is through the physical reaction of an extremely sensitive "startle reflex." For example, when she's in a room and doesn't know that someone has come in, she has an exaggerated reaction. Her family knows not to come up behind her and say "boo!"

If we were traumatized in the womb because our birth mothers were abused, mentally challenged, or on drugs, we may have sensory issues. Things are constantly firing in our brains. We can hear the slightest things, and to us, they sound so loud that we cover our ears.

Lois, a late-discovery adoptee, believes the major reason for the hypervigilance she experiences in adulthood was a contentious relationship with her adoptive father. "He wanted me to be his *biological* child," she explains. "So even though I didn't know that, there was a tension and a pressure to try to please him. I just didn't succeed because I couldn't. I was always afraid and said to myself, 'Is he going to be mad? What can I do?'"

Lois's innate belief system told her that dads are supposed to love their daughters. When she found in her dad only disappointment that she wasn't his biological child, fingernails scraped over the blackboard of her tender adopted soul.

Authors John and Paula Sanford say, "In the womb, every adopted child has in his spirit experienced rejection from his natural parents. He may have been reacting in his spirit with resentment, *tightening up* in defensiveness. Certainly rest and trust are not formed in him."[6]

Another indication that we are experiencing mixed feelings is an undercurrent of anxiety.

Anxiety

I resonate with what author Selma Fraiberg says about adoptee anxiety:

> Can a baby under one 'remember' this traumatic separation from his original parents? No, he probably will not remember the events as a series of pictures that can be recalled. What is remembered, or preserved, is anxiety, a primitive kind of terror, which returns in waves in later life.[7]

Many of us experience anxiety but may never associate it with adoption loss. "Oh, I'm just a nervous-type person," we may say to ourselves.

Sue Coons, adopted at nine months and found by her birth mother fifteen years ago at age forty-three, says that she developed a panic disorder when she was eight years old and never really understood it or had treatment until she was in her thirties. It was very difficult for her to deal with and created troublesome limitations in both her personal and professional life. She couldn't travel at all.

Lois Rabey links her hypervigilance with anxiety. She says that on an emotional level she has worried excessively about what might happen in the future to those she loves, from the present to years and years ahead. She tried everything to rid herself of the worry. Prayer. Meditation. Counseling. All to no avail.

When she became a grandmother she grew more and more exhausted with worry about her grandchildren and other family members. Overwhelmed with anxiety, she made a choice and said to God that she was going to commit all that she was worrying about to Him and intentionally let go of it every time it came up again. That decision has eased her hypervigilance and anxiety over time.

Words and statements that often produce painful feelings

Cognitive dissonance occurs automatically and involuntarily for many adoptees, but adoptive parents and other people in an adopted child's life can inadvertently trigger mixed feelings.

I believe that, for the most part, the following types of statements are well intentioned and born out of ignorance; nevertheless, they can have negative repercussions in an adoptee's mind and heart.

"How do you fix her hair?"

Tiffany Williams Savage, awesome mom to five children, says, "People always want to touch my black daughter's hair." She says she wants to get a shirt for her daughter that says, "Don't touch my hair!" Tiffany says that she has to be a voice for her children until they can find their voices. Love that.

"Are they twins?"

Suppose you're an adoptive mom of three, like Tiffany. One child is white, the other mixed race, and the third, dark black. People will say these kinds of things in front of her children: "Her skin is kind of white...oh, her skin is so, so dark. Are they siblings? Are their moms on drugs? Biologically, are they related?"

Her young adopted children's response? "You're my mommy, right?"

Tiffany stands up for them by saying, "You don't have to try to figure out our family."

"You're going to adopt another black child?"

"This black child isn't going to be like the one on the other side of town, is he?"

Ouch! Our extended adoptive family may be downright prejudiced. In the southern US, racism can still seep in, especially with comments like these. And it is certainly not just in the US: Shefalie Chandra experienced racism in the UK as a mixed-race person, with both Indian and Scottish ancestry. Her skin color made her stand out among the kids at school and she became the brunt of bullying.

"You're fulfilling the biblical mandate to adopt"

James 1:27 says to care for widows and orphans, but it doesn't say to marry off the widows and adopt orphans. Not everyone who claims to be a person of faith is called to parent an adopted child. Currently, repercussions of this trend are that many parents have changed their minds. It's harder than they anticipated. There are many disrupted adoptions.

Personally, I would never want to be someone's ministry. We simply want to be our parent's child. This religious attitude would be a barrier to my attachment to that parent.

"Your birth mother loved you so much that she gave you to us"

Trying to equate love and abandonment just doesn't work! I am reminded of the song that says, "Love and marriage, love and marriage…go together like a horse and carriage." What if we changed the phrase "love and marriage" to "love and abandonment"? Sing with me now: "Love and abandonment, love and abandonment, go together like a horse and carriage…"

Rather ridiculous, isn't it? Is it any wonder that being told that love is what led to our relinquishment produces mixed feelings? Yes, there may have been a loving adoption plan, but to most of us, separation from our birth mothers translates as rejection and abandonment, pure and simple.

Connie Dawson says it translates like this: "I love you/ go away." "Your birth mother loved you so much; she made a loving plan…blah, blah, blah." Or, "Your needs are important/ don't search for your birth parents or you'll hurt me."

Dr. Gregory C. Keck says:

I think it just confuses kids when people tell them that their birth mothers didn't keep them because they loved them.

I think it makes the kids feel even more responsible for inconveniencing their mothers by being born. Also, I think they must feel bad (guilty) about feeling bad, sad, lonely, or abandoned. After all, if someone did this because they loved them, what gives them the right to feel whatever they feel? Also, I think it makes 'loving' someone difficult since love is what 'got rid' of them. If their mothers loved them so much, should they have any negative feelings? Should they love her that much? I do wonder if anything helps kids feel better. Is it better or worse to be 'dumped' by a loving mother than by a hating, abusive, or terrible one?[8]

"You were chosen!"

Adoption experts Drs. David Brodzinsky and Marshall Schechter say:

> It has long been popular in adoption circles to emphasize that the adopted child is a *wanted* child or, as in the title of Wasson's 1939 classic children's book on adoption, *A Chosen Baby*. This emphasis is a fairly straightforward piece of denial: usually a child is available for adoption only because he was *unwanted*. It is no accident that Wasson's story neglects to mention the existence of *biological* parents. It is not an easy task to change an unwanted child into a wanted child. This challenge is, however, exactly the task faced by adoptive parents. They must convey to their adopted child that, although he was born to other parents who didn't want him, he is now their beloved child and shall always remain so.[9]

Lori says that she just couldn't believe the line, "You were a chosen child; nobody could love a kid more." She knew that her parents had adopted her in a last-ditch attempt to save their ailing marriage.

A poem by Mi Ok Song Bruining sums up the chosen-child dilemma:

They Said

They said
   Smile for the camera
   Open your eyes, they are squinting.
They said
   Stop crying, stop feeling bad.
   Those kids who call you "Chink"
   And "Flat Face"
   Don't know anything
   Besides, you probably provoked them.
They said
   Feel lucky
   You were "chosen"
   Really meaning
   I was also given up.
They said
   We are offended,
   You have everything, so be happy.
   Be appreciative, and
   Never let the tears show.
They said
   You don't belong here.
   Where do you come from?
   Do you speak English?
   Do you like America?
   As if I just landed
   From a distant galaxy.
They said
   Everything I hoped and dreamed
   And prayed they wouldn't.
   They still do.[10]

"Accentuate the positive!"

Another statement that sometimes causes mixed feelings is "accentuate the positive." You know—count your blessings, count them one by one. As I've spoken with hundreds of adoptees all over the country, I've discovered that this message is particularly common in religious families.

A well-meaning parent, church or synagogue member, or member of the clergy can unintentionally inflict harm by focusing exclusively on the many positive aspects of adoption while denying the negative and/or mixed feelings many adoptees have.

In the past, places of worship weren't adoption-sensitive. Adoption wasn't mentioned. People didn't recognize that adoption is a *mixed* blessing, filled with pleasure as well as pain. Instead, they looked at adoption through rose-colored glasses, trying to make it a win/win situation for unplanned pregnancies and infertility, never giving a thought about what effect adoption has on the child.

Currently, there are wonderful changes afoot, beginning in the US with adoption support programs and training. Drs. Karyn Purvis and David Cross at TCU Institute of Child Development have developed an emerging intervention model. So have Drs. Daniel Hughes and Joyce Macquire Pavao. Online growth groups abound. A huge evangelical movement in US, the Christian Alliance for Orphans (CAFO), hosts yearly summits with internationally known adoption speakers and experts. Hospital-based "adoption-sensitive" training programs have begun under the tutelage of Rebecca Swan Vahle's Family to Family Support Network, Inc., restoring honor to every member of the adoption triad (the birth mother, the adoptee and the adoptive parents) for infant adoptions.

At last…at last…the tide is turning positively…ever so slowly.

However, it is my belief that the adoptee's voice is still not heard publicly. At the time of this writing, we are still somewhat of a novelty.

Reflecting back, however, among those raised in the closed adoption era, eerie echoes of "accentuate the positive" keeps adoptees in bondage to the chaos inside. Ron Hilliard says that when others would try to affirm the positive but he wasn't feeling positive in his own heart, he felt guilty and ashamed. It was confusing to him why his heart would not be in agreement with those who tried to accentuate how fortunate he was. Like the good adoptee, Ron never verbalized the negative— he just smiled and nodded at how "lucky" he was to have such wonderful adoptive parents who had rescued him from abandonment.

Scott D. Stephens, LISW, a post-adoption social worker from Cincinnati, knew something wasn't quite right in terms of what he was feeling, but he didn't have the words to describe his mixed emotions. The message was somehow communicated that being adopted was a positive blessing and that positive feelings were expected in response. His parents would say things like, "Isn't it wonderful that you were loved so much that your parents chose you?" or "How fortunate you are to have been adopted!"

While all this was true, Ron's heart never quite believed it. All the emphasis on the positive never allowed room for the painful. As a result, the pain was never validated.

"You are special"

Another finger-over-the-blackboard statement claims that we are "special." I believe many adoptive parents intuitively know, even though most of them are not informed, that we are grieving. In perhaps an unconscious attempt to comfort us they may use this phrase. Others who are not educated about how an adoptee thinks and feels may do the same.

Some of us receive the statement with pride and gain a sense of self-worth. However, to many it means:

- Others have high expectations of us.

- We must prove our worth by excelling.

- We're not like everyone else in the family…we're different.

- Perform!

- Be perfect.

- Conform! Conform! Conform!

- It's not okay to just be ourselves.

Paula Oliver says that she can remember raising her hand in elementary school and telling everyone that she was adopted. Later on in the playground the kids made fun of her by saying stuff like, "Your mom didn't want you so she threw you away." Paula says:

> I ran into the school crying and was found by a teacher who told me that being adopted made me special because my parents *chose* me, while most parents are *stuck* with their kids! That was little comfort—it was more like a burden because I didn't feel special.

Whenever I teach this point during training, many parents get upset. "Can't I tell my child she is special?" My answer is always, "Of course, but not in regard to adoption."

"We love you just like our own"

Adoptive parents think they are giving us a great compliment with these words, but more than often, they wound. When well-meaning parents say, "We love you *just like* you're our own," their child may naturally wonder or hopefully ask, *Well, if I'm not your own, then whose am I? Where is my real family? Where do I belong?* The parents' statements often translate as "You're *really not* our own. *Almost*, but not completely."

Says one adoptee, "I can't stand it when people differentiate between biological and adopted kids. 'Oh, we have three of our own and then one adopted daughter.'"

What are healing words instead? "We have six children."

No singling out adoptees. We hate that and it hurts.

"You belong"

Another statement concerns our sense of belonging. Try this simple exercise. Fold your hands together as quickly as you can. Then look. Which thumb is on the top of the fold? Is it your right or left? Let's say, for example, it's your right thumb. Now do exactly the same exercise, at the same speed, but aim at getting your opposite thumb on the top of your fingers. Not as easy as the first time, is it?

The awkwardness in this simple exercise could be likened to many adoptees' feelings of not belonging. I can't tell you how many adoptees say in support groups, "I feel like an alien, like I wasn't born, like I was just dropped down to earth by a stork or something."

Connie Dawson has awareness of feelings such as of not belonging:

> I guess I'm a partial belonger...I was a good 'fitter in-ner' in my adoptive family, in which it was never a topic for discussion. Although I have been warmly received by my birth aunt, I don't really belong there either—at least not the way I imagine other people belong. When I'm visiting her, I feel accepted, but I notice she doesn't throw a family dinner when I visit. One of her nephews (my cousin) will call on the phone and I'm jealous of the endearing and warm

teasing they do with one another. I have this persistent feeling of not being entitled to *really* belong, to *really* take a seat at the table, to *really* be heard in a group, to *really* trust myself, to *really* trust others. You probably would be surprised to know this if you observed me in action, but I know I could be so much more.

Richard Curtis says that since he was a total surprise at his reunion, birth relatives gave various degrees of welcoming. He says he deluged them with questions about his birth parents, hungry to learn the details of his heritage. And then he thought to himself, *Now, where does Richard fit into the lives of these people? On the fringe.* "I have this deep need to bond with real blood relatives," he explains, "but I feel like I'm not really a part of either of my families."

Author Corrine Chilstrom, after learning that her eighteen-year-old adopted son committed suicide after leaving home for college, pounded her fist on the kitchen table shouting, "Adoption! These kids never feel like they really belong in this world. Who will ever understand?"[11]

For many, the preceding statements and words simply don't line up with what we believe in our heart of hearts is true. Like teenage kids at our first dance, we try so hard to have "good rhythm" with our dancing partners, but instead we seem to step all over their toes. But we can put an end to the awkwardness by making a better choice regarding our mixed feelings.

I can tell you, though, that it's taken a lifetime for me to get to that place. We need to be patient with ourselves. And we never "arrive!"

Our Choice

To claim both positive and painful emotions as valid and verbalize them.

Ron Hilliard describes our choice beautifully when he says, "As I have learned to accept both the positive as well as the negative, I now have opportunities to articulate both and can claim my mixed feelings as valid."

How to begin

If we still deny that our adoption experience produces mixed feelings, the healing won't begin. Here are some suggestions:

- *Record your current circumstances in a journal.* Draw a self-portrait. How about getting a huge piece of paper? Then, have someone trace your whole body. When the drawing is complete and you are alone, write down the conflicting feelings coming out of your head and heart. Draw the people and messages that are prompting them, and then label the physical effects on every part of your body. When you are done, title your portrait in big letters: "ALL OF MY FEELINGS ARE REAL AND OKAY!"

- *Create a collage out of old magazines and newspapers depicting your mixed feelings.* I remember cutting out a photo from a newspaper of a man who was weeping. He was a survivor of the Holocaust. I didn't know why I cut out the image, but looking back, I can now see that it was because it was how I was feeling inside. It would be thirty years later that I would learn that I am of Jewish descent! Our roots run wondrously deep.

- *Try to identify and then name the conflicting feelings,* record them, and then say aloud, "I am having mixed feelings, and that is perfectly normal and acceptable."

Now that we've learned about these finger-over-the-blackboard reactions, it is important that we educate ourselves about the dynamics within our adoptive families. We'll talk about that at some length in the next chapter.

The roots of education are bitter, but the fruit is sweet.

—ARISTOTLE

CHAPTER five

Learning about Adoption Dynamics Will Help Us Relax

Imagine a sunny Florida beach with a hot and dusty boardwalk leading down to the ocean. You slip on your sandals and walk the length of the boardwalk. As you near the end, you notice several empty pairs of shoes scattered along the boardwalk's edge. Shoes of all sizes, styles, and shapes. Each pair unique. Each bearing the imprint of its owner's feet. Each with a story to tell.

You realize you've never walked in another person's shoes. Never have. Never will. The same is true in adoption. There are several pairs of adoption shoes sitting at the end of the boardwalk. The adoptee's...the birth parents'...and the adoptive or foster parents'. Each is unique and each has a story to tell.

Like the sunbather realizing he will never wear another person's shoes, we, in the adoption triad, must respect the fact that we will never completely understand each other's pain or joy. However, through education, we can walk together for a while. By walking side by side instead of apart, we will grow in our capacity to love and be loved. Education enables us to do that.

You are cordially invited
To join a new
All-Adoptee Growth Group Meeting online!
Only adoptees belong
And here, you will find a safe place
To share your journey
Without fear of judgment.

Please RSVP to Sherrie
As soon as possible!

(All-Adoptees@yahoogroups.com)

Back in the day, television talk-show host Oprah Winfrey hosted a book club motivating millions to begin reading thought-provoking literature. She selected the book and challenged her viewers to read it. At the end, she chose six to eight women who had also read and enjoyed the book to join her in her home for a candlelit dinner and a cozy talk about the book.

Like Oprah and many others, I have discovered the incredible benefits of education. Books take us outside of ourselves and invite us into the world of another person, or people, where we can learn new viewpoints. We become more developed people who can identify with others who aren't just like us.

During this chapter, we can have our own little book club. Want to join? Just imagine yourself seated around my dining room table, eating a delicious meal with me and fellow adoptees, talking about our favorite books. The people who will be around the table will share their excitement in learning about adoption and also the books that they found most helpful. Their favorite books will give you ideas for when you visit your local library or bookstore.

Years ago, I was not a reader. But, after going back to college in my mid-forties to finish my undergraduate degree, I was given an assignment for a creative writing class that required that I weave a few facts around research-based fiction. I knew immediately what my topic would be—adoption. I had the few facts about my adoption and would study the times of my birth and weave fiction around them. I was astounded to find that there was an *entire section* in the university library devoted to the subject of adoption!

While sequestered in a reading booth, I'll never forget digging through the archived magazines and research articles, looking for nitty-gritty aspects of life in the 1940s—clothing, cars, food, magazines, and advertisements. Finding this information made it possible for me to dream about what it must have been like during the time when my birth mother carried me.

An interesting phenomenon began as I delved into these books and articles. Thoughts sounded familiar. Emotions rang true. Issues were similar. And much to my astonishment I found *myself* in those pages through the lives of other adoptees! I felt drawn to adoption literature, like a fish to water.

Renee Mills, a reunited adoptee who was born one week after legislators sealed adoption records, is a great example. Once she started reading, she couldn't stop! She had no idea that so much was written about her *own* life experience. Renee says, "I felt validated because someone *finally* put a name on the lifelong thoughts and feelings I had been unable to verbalize. For once in my life I felt understood and free to be myself!"

Her favorite books are *The Primal Wound* by Nancy Verrier and *Lost and Found* by Betty Jean Lifton.

The benefits of self-education

Let's take a look at four reasons why our fellow adoptees are fired up about reading adoption literature. (And keep in mind that when some of them mention my first book, I didn't pay them to do so!)

"I finally understand my adoptive parents"

I distinctly remember walking the beaches of Destin, Florida, one warm summer day, thinking about my relationship with my adoptive parents. I was in the depths of counseling and examining why a sense of distance existed between my parents and me in my growing-up years. There was an unexplainable sadness that hung over our family, like a dark cloud before a storm.

I subconsciously translated this sadness as disappointment in *me*, even though there was no logical basis for it. My parents would have done anything for me...in fact, perhaps too much. Frankly, anything little Sherrie wanted, little Sherrie got. So this unspoken sadness...where did it come from?

That day on the beach, after having read a lot about adoption, I realized that my parents had never grieved their many years of infertility. This is a common issue in adoption—an "adoption dynamic." Knowing the era in which they experienced this, with no literature about adoption available, they couldn't have understood this dynamic. They were doing the best they could. How freeing it was for me to learn this! The unresolved sadness in our home wasn't about me...it was about them. Knowing this, I was able to love and appreciate them even more, even though both of them had passed away.

"I know I am not alone"

Remember, we're still around the table. Still talking about adoption dynamics, and someone says, "You felt that way most of your life too?"

What do you think they might have been talking about? Here's a clue: it's one of the secrets we keep well hidden behind our "strong" façades.

You guessed it…loneliness.

Many of us have carried that secret for years. Even though we may have many acquaintances or friends, we still may feel lonely. This can be equally true of non-adoptees, but I think because of adoptees' "mixed feelings" discussed in Chapter Four, it may be a heavier burden for us.

Connie Dawson says she didn't begin to get educated until she and her husband of twenty-four years divorced, and she read *Lost and Found* by Betty Jean Lifton. "It was a marvel to find out someone else felt so many of the feelings I did!" Connie says.

Phyllis-Anne Munro, a social worker who has been reunited with both birth parents, says that the books she read helped her know that she was not alone in this journey. Some of the books that have rocked her world are *The Primal Wound* by Nancy Verrier; *Journey of the Adopted Self: A Quest for Wholeness* by Betty Jean Lifton; *The Secret Thoughts of an Adopted Mother* by Jana Wolff; *The Other Mother* by Carol Schaefer; and *I Hope You Have a Good Life* by Campbell Armstrong.

Despite Richard Curtis's concentrated work in dealing with his addictions, the topic of adoption was never discussed with his therapists or in any group setting. The resulting frustration led him to the local library where he located his first adoption-related book: *Being Adopted: The Lifelong Search for Self* by Drs. David Brodzinsky and Marshall Schechter. "I was overwhelmed, finding myself described within the pages of this book. I no longer felt alone," Richard says.

Ron Hilliard began listening to tapes about adoption that gave voice to what he already was feeling.

> I began to realize that there were a large number of people who had the same experience as I did. I had always felt alone in my adoption world, and now I discovered that I was no longer alone. I discovered that while each adoptee's experience is unique, there are also common threads amongst us. The most helpful books were *Twenty Things Adopted Kids Wish Their Adoptive Parents Knew* by Sherrie Eldridge and Ron Nydam's *Adoptees Come of Age*.

Seven-year-old Maggie Backiewicz of Ohio, who enjoys piano, Girl Scouts, and an open adoption, says that her favorite adoption book is *A Koala for Katie*, by Jonathan London and Cynthia Jabar. And why does she like to read it? Because if she forgets, the book reminds her that other kids are adopted too.

Erika Hill lives in Southern California with her family and enjoys reading and taking adventurous trips. She says:

> Before I read anything about adoptees, I was alone in a way that I didn't even realize. The more I read, the more astonished I was to find that most of my feelings were common among adoptees. Now I am almost narcissistically drawn to adoption literature. My favorite books are *May the Circle Be Unbroken: An Intimate Journey into the Heart of Adoption* by Lynn C. Franklin with Elizabeth Ferber and *Journey of the Adopted Self* by Betty Jean Lifton.

Lisa Storms echoes the same theme of finding out she was not alone in her feelings about adoption. "Every time I read an adoptee's account of the myriad of emotions [he or she has] dealt with in being adopted, I could totally relate. I stopped feeling 'different' and realized that we share many aspects of our journey."

Sharon McGowan, adopted at six weeks of age and reunited with her birth mother nine years ago, has read all the adoption books she could get her hands on over the years:

I felt like I was alone in my 'issues' and that something was very wrong with me, but after reading the first few books, I understood how adoption contributed to my 'issues' and that I was in good company. I was, in a word, relieved! The first book about adoption I read was *Lost and Found* by Betty Jean Lifton, but I think *The Primal Wound* by Nancy Verrier was one of the best.

"I feel compassion for birth mothers"

Another exciting aspect of learning about adoption is that we can walk awhile in the shoes of our birth parents. I believe full healing and redemption cannot occur for us as adoptees until we understand how birth parents feel. We first must look at our own pain, but that's only the beginning of the restoration. We need to realize that we weren't the only ones who felt rejected or abandoned or who had mixed feelings—many birth parents do too.

"Never in my life did I think about the pain that birth parents go through when they relinquish their babies," Michelle says. "Now, after meeting some birth parents and reading some birth parent stories, I have a better appreciation of their pain. We are all in this together!"

Sandy Garrett says it was truly an eye-opener to read the thoughts of birth mothers. She appreciates support groups where she can see first hand the pain in the eyes of birth mothers:

Now, that was an education for me… It made me feel like I was that much closer to my birth mother. Now I know that there was a reason behind my adoption. I met a woman who gave up her child and felt pain every single day of her life because of it. It made the people in my life—me, my birth mom, and my adoptive parents—that much more human. My favorite books are *The Primal Wound* by Nancy Vernier; *Twenty Things Adopted Kids Wish Their Adoptive Parents Knew* by Sherrie Eldridge; *When to Forgive* by Mona Gustafson, Ph.D.; and *Reunion: A Year in Letters between a Birthmother and the Daughter She Couldn't Keep* by Katie Hern and Ellen McGarry Carlson.

Jodi Strathman has educated herself endlessly in the last two years and attended her first American Adoption Congress (AAC) where she saw all sides of the triad. She's come to understand that while the circumstances in each adoption are different, the emotional repercussions are similar.

Annual conventions of adoption organizations are a great way to educate ourselves. Paige Wilson of California says education was extremely helpful because it gave her a perspective about the adoption triad that she lacked. *The Adoption Triangle: The Effects of the Sealed Records on Adoptees, Birth Parents, and Adoptive Parents* by Arthur Sorosky gave her insight not only into her own behavior, but also that of her birth and adoptive parents. "I have always tried to educate myself about adoption even from an early age," says Kim Pittsley. "My favorite book is Hern and Carlson's volume of letters written by birth mothers to the children they placed. The outpouring of raw emotion and unconditional love in those letters gave me a profound respect for the choices that my birth and adoptive parents made and the strong people that they are."

"I have a new sense of freedom"

After we find new understanding of our birth and adoptive parents and discover how loneliness need no longer be our primary emotional reality, a wonderful new sense of freedom comes.

Frieda Moore says that she didn't have a clue that there was anything to be educated about concerning her experience of being adopted. But with reading came freedom, and she is now very comfortable with who she is. She says that *Twenty Things Adopted Kids Wish Their Adoptive Parents Knew* was a "heart opener" and "hit the nail on the head" in so many ways for her.

Brad says, "Educating myself about adoption through attending adoption support groups made me feel empowered concerning adoption-related conversations, whereas before I was uncomfortable and unable to speak intelligently about my adoption and the feelings associated with being an adoptee."

If you've never educated yourself about the dynamics of adoption, I hope this chapter has whetted your appetite and brought you to the threshold of making another life-enhancing choice for yourself. We can choose to remain where we are in our knowledge about adoption, or we can be seekers and communicators of truth, looking for every opportunity to educate ourselves and enjoy the freedom that comes with deeper understanding.

Our Choice

To educate ourselves about adoption through reading adoption literature, joining webinars, and/or attending conventions and support groups.

How to begin

- *Attend an adoption convention.* I am only willing to recommend the conventions I have attended, which is why most of those listed are in the US, but there are many others that you will want to investigate and possibly attend.

+ The AAC was my first experience at a convention and it was life-changing. I never knew that there was an adoption world out there, filled with people whose lives had been touched by adoption. There is always a plethora of seminars to attend and dynamic keynote speeches.

+ The Association for Treatment and Training in the Attachment of Children (ATTACh) is a group of parents and professionals who are trying to help children with attachment disorders and difficulties with adoption-related matters.

+ The North American Council for Adoptable Children (NACAC) is an awesome organization that probably has the most dynamic and diverse program of any. Its convention is held annually.

+ The Christian Alliance for Orphans (CAFO) is a dynamic group of evangelicals who are passionate about adoption, foster care, and orphan care. They have yearly summits and state-wide support. They also have a blog.

• Outside of the US, I'd recommend contacting organizations such as The British Association for Adoption and Fosterity in the UK and ReachOut in Australia as well as Holt International for worldwide services.

• *Adoption blogs.* I recommend Lori Lavender Luz for an open-adoption perspective (http://lavenderluz.com).

- *Google "adoption" and see what comes up!* You won't believe all that is available and how much of it is free online.

- *Be on the lookout for new books on the topic.* E-books are inexpensive.

- *Order teaching tapes.* If you aren't able to attend an international convention, check out organizations' sites to see if they offer tapes of the sessions. More than likely they do, so even if you miss a convention, you can glean all the information that was provided.

- *Attend local seminars.*

- *Subscribe to online magazines or newsletters.*

- *Orphan Sunday and Adoption Awareness Month* both occur in November in the US—the same month as National Adoption Week in the UK and National Adoption Awareness Week in Australia. Think about reading a children's adoption book at your local bookstore or library. Perhaps hold a candlelit vigil for the children in your city who don't have permanent homes yet.

I'm sure you can add many ideas to the list, but this will get you started!

So lonely 'twas, that God himself scarce seemed there to be.

—COLERIDGE

CHAPTER six

It May Often Seem like No One "Gets It"

Have you ever let yourself be totally transparent to someone about an adoption-related topic or issue and have that person look at you like you had just stepped off a spaceship? It could be a friend, a spouse, an in-law, a colleague, a parent, a therapist, a physician…anyone.

We try so hard to be understood and to connect, but more often than not our basic need isn't met. Adoption experts Drs. David Brodzinsky and Marshall Schechter say that adoptees have "a driven need for human connectedness. This craving grows with time, experienced subjectively by some adoptees as equivalent to starvation."[1]

We need to connect with others about our experience but it's like we're speaking a different language. It reminds me of a time years ago when my husband's family hosted a German foreign exchange student. Upon arrival he couldn't speak a word of English. They did various things to help him understand—hand motions, charades, talking louder, then louder…but nothing worked.

It's often the same with us, isn't it, when we're trying to communicate our feelings about adoption. We're often misunderstood.

The Synonym Finder tells us that to misunderstand is to "misapprehend, misread, misjudge, miscalculate, miscount, misreckon, read it wrong, get it all wrong, get a false impression, miss the point, see through a glass darkly."[2] To be misunderstood is a disconcerting experience for anyone, but for adoptees it can be particularly hurtful.

Many wounds in life are easy to name. "My mother died when I was five." "I was sexually abused by my brother." "I became a widow a few months ago." But for the majority of us adoptees, our trauma occurred soon after birth when we didn't have the ability to describe our wounds. We had only sensations and feelings.

I believe that our ability to communicate the feelings associated with that trauma remains at an infant stage, and when we get too close to pain, tears or anger often come easier than words. We may want to curl up in a fetal position and die, pack our bags and run away, or scream at the top of our lungs in utter frustration. We just don't know what to do with ourselves, let alone communicate what is bothering us to someone else.

Martha says she has adoptive parents and friends who are supportive, but do they "get it"? No! Compounding the problem is that she doesn't "get it" either. She believes her friends might understand more if she could find the words to express it better.

Sandy Garrett, who has been reunited with her birth mom for two years, appreciates her husband's attempts to communicate understanding but the reality is that she feels constantly misunderstood. "Plain and simple," she says, "he just doesn't get it."

Kim Norman, happily married mother of two who has been searching for her birth mother for four years in New York, says that when she was waiting for the results of a court order to open her records in another state, she asked everyone she knew to say a little prayer for her, and the response was either silence or dismay at why she would be so "overly concerned" about such an "insignificant" matter.

Paula Oliver remembers when she first bared her heart about the thing we all struggle with—fear of rejection from our birth parents. Paula has met hers, yet when she verbalized this fear with whom she considered to be good friends, they put a Band-Aid over her wound with a platitude: "I'm sure they did it because they thought it was the best thing for you."

Ouch!

Imagine a world where all the people who care about us read every adoption book they could get their hands on. Everyone would ooze with empathy and understanding, and we would feel connected as never before. Wouldn't that be wonderful?

Only in our dreams! The majority of people we know are not going to become book hounds on adoption-related matters. And so, what's the answer? Do we continue in our feelings of frustration, hurt, disappointment, and disillusionment? Do we isolate ourselves further from well-meaning friends and family members who are only trying to help?

Of course not!

As adoptees, we need to learn to not take the "not get it" responses personally. If we don't learn to do this, we will become stuck in anger, resentment, and bitterness.

I have come to believe that the raw feelings we experience when working through adoption issues are a rite of passage we must work through, not stay in. So many of us are stuck. That's not what we want.

There is a better way. We can work with an attachment therapist for post-adoption issues and when misunderstood by outsiders, we must learn to set healthy boundaries. There is method called W.I.S.E. Up!® that was developed by Marilyn Schoettle, MA.[3] It was designed for children and teens, but I believe it can be equally effective for adults. There is now a version for foster children. I've used it myself and it works.

The W.I.S.E. Up!® method is taught through the use of the acronym: W.I.S.E. Here's what each letter stands for:

W—WALK AWAY

I—IT'S PRIVATE

S—SHARE

E—EDUCATE

Each option is a way we can first take care of ourselves when misunderstood, and at the same time teach others.

While this is not a guarantee that others will understand or want to understand, it is a guarantee that by becoming proactive instead of passive when well-intentioned, ignorant, insensitive, or crass remarks come our way, we will slowly regain a sense of control in our lives.

Walk away

The first choice involves the big "W." We can simply walk away when others misunderstand…but walk away without anger. That is the challenge.

How many of us ever think about options when misunderstood? If you're anything like me, I get so caught up in anger or hurt that the thought of an option never enters my mind (uh-oh…there's that victim mentality again).

But now that we know we have options, we can take a deep breath and think, "W, W, W, W, W, W!" The "walk away" option provides maximum self-care and communicates a strong message to the sender: "Your remarks were inappropriate and hurtful."

The kids in Brad's class teased, "You don't have any real parents. You don't even know who your parents are. You don't even have the same color skin as them." According to the acronym, which of the four options should Brad choose?

If I were Brad, I would definitely choose "W"—especially if he was feeling vulnerable at the time.

Cheri Freeman describes a "walk away time" in her life: "Once I asked my husband's family for their cooperation in writing a book about their collective adoptive experiences. One sister stood up and pretty much told me that if I thought their story was worth telling, I couldn't be much of a writer."

Phyllis-Anne Munro describes a "tune-up visit" to what she termed her "treasured therapist of many years." She made an appointment to read a letter she was about to send to her birth mother. In an unexpected turn of events, the therapist proceeded to read her the riot act by saying that even "normal birth families" don't sit around and discuss aunts and uncles or cancer and diabetes. Phyllis-Anne says, "I felt belittled and invalidated. Then I felt really angry! It was disheartening and I have not sought her out again."

See how powerful the choice to walk away can be? Victim thinking and behavior fades and healthy self-care begins.

It's private

The second option—"it's private"—also provides protection, yet communicates and educates. A time that we might choose to say "it's private" is when relatives or friends learn that we're initiating a search for birth relatives. Someone may say, "Why would you want to do THAT?" Or, "Why would you want to open THAT can of worms?"

What can we do? We can simply smile and say, "It's private. I really don't feel like talking about it right now."

Another example would be concerning those who were adopted at an older age because of serious parental neglect or abuse. "Isn't it wonderful that you have a new family?" someone may say. The adoptee's response could be: "That's a private subject."

Share

The third letter in the acronym, "S", stands for "share." This begins the opening-up process in which we let others hear our feelings and beliefs on a limited basis.

Richard Curtis might have chosen this in the following situation:

> The people who seem to least understand how my relinquishment and adoption have affected me are my adult children. At one point, I eagerly awaited the opportunity to relate new information about my birth family. I'll never forget the looks on their faces when I explained the results of my search and showed them pictures of my birth father. They asked a few questions, were surprised about our Italian background, but showed no further enthusiasm.

Richard says he felt like he'd been slapped in the face. Using the W.I.S.E. Up!® method, he might share with his grown up, apathetic children, "Someday I know that your kids are going to want to know about their family history, so I'm going to write it down and preserve it for them and future generations."

When Sandy Garrett told her husband that she was going to search for her birth mother, her husband pooh-poohed the idea, asking why she would want to search for another mother—she already had one and that should be good enough.

Okay, Sandy...choose "S"! "I have always felt like there is a missing piece of the puzzle in my life. It's very important for me to find that piece through searching."

Even though she has since been reunited with her birth mother, her husband still asks her on a regular basis why she wants to go to her adoption support group. "S" again, Sandy!

"I need to be with other adoptees and hear their experiences. It helps me stay in touch with my own feelings."

Educate

"E" for "educate"—the last letter of the acronym—it involves risk but pays great dividends. Here we educate, but only when we are strong, both emotionally and spiritually.

Sharon McGowan says her closest friends either got defensive, insisting that she shouldn't be dwelling on her adoptee status, or dismissive, telling her not to "play the victim." "And these are people who love me!" Sharon says with dismay.

Sharon might seize this opportunity to educate her judgmental friends by saying, "Did you know that adoption experts say that adoptees are victims of the gravest kind? We had those initial bonds of trust broken at birth."

Sharon also says that her birth mother incessantly apologizes or takes herself on a guilt trip by saying things like, "I know all of your problems are my fault." In response to her guilt-ridden birth mother, Sharon could educate: "Did you know that many birth mothers feel the same way as you? Placing a child for adoption is one of the most agonizing decisions a woman can ever make. There is a wonderful book that could help you get rid of that guilt; it's called *The Other Mother*, by Carol Schaefer. There's probably a copy at the library."

"Wising up" as adoptees involves practicing new ways of responding to the misunderstandings of others about our adoption experiences.

It's educational to others, but not at our expense. Instead of our adoptee fantasy of our loved ones delving into adoption books, we become the books they read!

I am reminded of a story about the famous pianist, Ignacy Paderewski, who was scheduled to perform at a black-tie affair at a great concert hall. Present in the audience was a mother and her fidgety nine-year-old son, who was brought against his wishes in hopes that he would be inspired to practice more.

Before the performance, when the mother turned to talk to friends, the boy slipped out of his seat, walked onstage to the Steinway piano, and began playing "Chopsticks." The crowd was extremely irritated and various people yelled, "Get that boy away from there! Who'd bring a kid that young in here? Where's his mother? Somebody stop him."

Backstage the master overheard the sounds, figured out what was happening, grabbed his coat, and rushed on to the stage. Without a word, he stooped over behind the boy and reached around both sides, improvising a countermelody to harmonize and enhance "Chopsticks." And as he did, he whispered in the boy's ears, "Don't quit, son! Keep going. Keep on playing."

Sometimes we are like the boy on the stage of our lives being booed by insensitive people around us who "just don't get it" and who tire of our talk about adoption. But I have found that if we just keep practicing, even if we can only play "Chopsticks," the master will hurry onstage, bend over us, play a countermelody, and say to us, "Don't quit! Keep on going. Keep on trying."

We don't have to be sitting ducks any longer! We can walk away from being a victim by not setting ourselves up for misunderstanding and by taking responsibility for our actions. It's time for us to grow up. Each offense is an invitation for growth.

Our Choice

To be proactive instead of passive when others misunderstand or mistreat us.

We've covered a lot of territory in this chapter, so let's make sure the information we gleaned gets appropriated. Here are some suggestions.

How to begin

- *Make a list of all the misunderstanding comments you can remember from childhood until the present.* Draw two lines down the middle of a clean sheet of paper, separating it into three columns. Put these titles over the columns: *Misunderstanding, How I Responded to them, How I Would Respond Today.* Use the W.I.S.E Up!® method.

- *Make a list of positive thoughts and affirmations you can memorize* that will keep you from becoming angry when offended. For example:

  + I will take a deep breath and remember I have a choice about how to respond.

  + I will tell myself that I'm learning one of the most important lessons of life—to not take things personally.

  + I will see the big picture of my life.

  + The deep hurts are your rite of passage to maturity. We're meant to pass through, not live there. Don't be afraid of the dark. You will come through this in glowing colors. I am cheering you on!

Just as we need to be W.I.S.E. in dealing with misunderstanding, we also need to learn to whom we can bare our hearts. Who is "safe"? We'll talk about that in detail in the following chapter.

We all need to know what it is that we are looking to confront and to avoid. If you are going to give your heart to people and trust them, you have to know what you are looking for.

—DR. HENRY CLOUD

CHAPTER **seven**

Share Deep Feelings Only With "Safe" People

Finding "safe" people has been a tough life lesson for me. This is a part of my story that I rarely share, but I write in the hope that it may encourage those of you who are really hurting and struggling with depression.

When we moved from Michigan to Indianapolis, I was hurting, big time. Of course, geographical moves can trigger abandonment issues for adoptees. Left behind were family members, a class of women I loved leading, and everything familiar.

Prior to moving, I believed and taught that depression isn't such a big deal, and that anyone who has it can choose to pull themselves up by the bootstraps and go on. Sadly, I looked down on those who couldn't get past depression.

The move to Indianapolis was so difficult for me that I sought counseling. But it didn't help. The first counselor told me that if I would just do this and then that, I'd be fine. All my troubles would go away. So, being the good little adoptee, I tried as hard as I could to believe and conform to what this guy said, but my mood continued to spiral downwards.

Isolation became my daily choice. Bob would kiss me goodbye before going to work and mention one single thing he'd like me to do during the day. I sat in my chair in the bedroom, staring out my window until he got home. Weight started falling off me at an incredible rate. I felt painfully self-conscious and anxious. Making decisions seemed impossible. What to wear, what to eat for lunch, and what to say?

On one particular morning, I decided to go for a walk to a neighbor's house. She took one look at me and told me she'd like to come home with me and call Bob to come home. She was a nurse and knew what hallucinations were.

When Bob arrived, he was understandably upset. He'd spent hour upon hour listening to me, to no avail. I know he felt helpless. What had happened to the one he had always called "his beautiful wife?"

When the neighbor left, Bob called our family physician and we drove in for an emergency appointment. As she examined me and asked questions, it seemed like she was in another room, her voice was so faint. It was then that she suggested Bob and I go to a psychiatrist and she made arrangements for an immediate appointment.

Seated in the doctor's office, his feet looked as though they were four feet long. Strange. It was after asking questions that he recommended I be hospitalized for clinical depression.

Bob and I were terrified. We'd never been to a counselor before our move to Indianapolis. Our youngest daughter, then in high school, came as I was checked into the local stress center.

Upon checking in, the nurse asked if I had considered taking my life. "I've thought about it but would never do it," I answered. That remark qualified me for the lock-down psychiatric unit.

The psychiatrist who evaluated me suggested medication. Bob called the first counselor I told you about and he told us that taking medicine for depression was a sin. I took it anyway.

Then, the three of us were ushered into a small room and the nurse asked extensive questions. I felt so deep-down guilty for putting my husband and daughter through that. I watched tears stream down their cheeks.

Finally, I was shown to a room and later it was time for my husband and daughter to leave. As I saw them headed toward the door, I panicked. Then the door opened and they were gone from sight.

I ran after them and tried to open the locked doors, at which time an attendant came and announced to me that the doors were locked for a purpose—to keep me safe.

After that, I curled up in a fetal position on the couch, wishing I could die.

That night, they gave me five shots of anti-psychotic drugs so that I could sleep. It had been five nights that I'd had no sleep whatsoever. The next morning, I was back to reality. A hospitalized social worker wept when he saw me come to breakfast the next morning. He was sure after seeing me the previous night that I might never recover.

For ten long days I was in that place. I hated it. The first night, a nude lady ran screaming through the unit. What was I doing there? I tried to talk with staff about what I thought might be causing my depression and there was no connection with them whatsoever. I literally had to put one foot in front of the other. Heaven seemed shut to me. I couldn't hear the comforting sound of the nightingale.

People didn't know what to say. There was a lot of whispering. What do you do when someone is in the situation I was in? The late Reverend Russ Blowers knew the right answer. He visited every day, sitting in a soft chair opposite me. He'd look me in the eyes, reach out his hands to hold mine, and then simply say, "How are you? Is there anything I can do for you today?" Before leaving, he prayed for me.

My late friend, Gary Rowe, M.Div., told me that being hospitalized for depression in a lock-down unit is the ultimate stripping of dignity. I totally agree.

I was released after ten days with the admonition to get counseling. After the first experience, I was hesitant. However, my dear friend Phyllis recommended someone she was seeing and I began seeing this woman on a weekly basis. Back in the day, there weren't adoption specialists, but she knew her stuff. It was through my work with her that I penned my first book and returned to university to finish my Bachelor's degree.

Wholeheartedly, I believe that doctors and medication can be part of a miraculous recovery. If I hadn't taken the meds, I might still be "checked out." I heard a story once about two seminary students who became clinically depressed. One took the medicine and the other refused, believing it was a sin. The first one recovered and went on to have a great life, while the second never regained mental health.

Depression can be the blues you get over in a few days, or it can be a life-threatening illness. I would learn that when hospitalized a few years later after being rejected by a cruel birth mother. I saw patients on IVs who were dying from depression. There should be no stigma about it, yet there is, and it hurts.

Reflecting on that experience has led me to examine various aspects of safety in relationships. What is safety? Who are safe people? How can we recognize them and subsequently develop rewarding friendships?

Why trust can be difficult for us

Before we discuss these questions, we need to examine two dilemmas that often prevent us from finding safe people and developing healthy relationships.

We often trust only ourselves

Drs. David Brodzinsky and Marshall Schechter say that the foundation for feeling safe depends on our ability to trust. "Trust allows an infant to feel he can depend on his own behavior as well as that of his caregivers. Without trust, he may grow up doubting his own self-worth, and doubting the motives of everyone he meets."[1]

Ahh…trust. The commodity we long for but few of us possess. Reflecting on Brodzinsky and Schechter's comments about the need for trust both in ourself *and* caregivers, do you think it possible that one half of the equation—learning to trust others—could be missing from our personal trust equations? Do you suppose it's possible that when we were separated from our first family, no matter our age, that we couldn't trust anyone but ourselves?

Sharon tests everyone in her life all the time, to prove to herself whether or not they can be trusted. The tests are never fair and she doesn't tell people they are being tested. When they fail, she is secretly glad because it proves her theory that no one can really care for her.

And what is the result of not learning to trust others? This brings us to our second dilemma.

We may be stuck emotionally

Erik Erikson, a German-born American psychoanalyst, was abandoned by his father before birth. Interestingly enough, some say he was almost obsessed with his theory of development (is it any wonder?), which postulates eight stages of development each characterized by a crisis that needs to be resolved. Here's how it works.

At the point of crisis the child is faced with a choice between coping in an adaptive or maladaptive way. Only as each crisis is resolved, which involves an evolution in personality, does the child have the strength to deal with the next stage of development. If a child does not resolve the conflict, he or she will confront and struggle with it later in life.[2] In other words, if we don't get it the first time around, we must go back and learn it.

Some of us already possess trust or may have revisited and resolved the conflict, but others may still have to face it someday. Crystal says she has always had a nagging suspicion that everyone in the world has something in them that makes them able to understand each other, to know what is *really* going on in relationships, and to give and receive love. "I have imagined that I don't have these abilities because I am adopted and missed the developmental stage where most people get blessed with these gifts."

If we never came through this crisis of trust as infants, do you think this means we will remain infants emotionally for the rest of our lives? Do we have to stay stuck?

Absolutely not!

Trust can be *learned*. If we haven't learned it from our initial caregiver (our birth mother or adoptive parents), we can learn it from others who have successfully passed through that stage of development and moved on toward maturity.

20 LIFE-TRANSFORMING CHOICES ADOPTEES NEED TO MAKE

Trust can be learned

Authors and Professors of Psychiatry Malcolm L. West and Adrienne E. Sheldon-Keller say:

> The securely attached adult can acknowledge felt distress in a modulated way and turn to supportive and trusted relationships for comfort. Particularly during periods of emotional upset, comfort often needs to be expressed in concrete attachment behaviors that reassure the individual. Put simply, felt security at these times has a lot to do with having someone available who will respond to our feelings and even take supportive action. The special warmth that often accompanies attachment comes just from these tangible reassurances that one is understood.[3]

Now let's translate this into adoptee terms and see how trust can be developed for adopted individuals.

Through a no-risk confidante

Connie Dawson has a rewarding trust relationship. She says:

> I don't share deep feelings with anyone unless I deem them to be a no-risk confidante. I can talk with other adoptees about adoption issues, but only to a point. If I want to go to a newly discovered place in myself that is related to adoption, I test out whether the other person can go there too. I am fortunate to have a fellow-traveler adoptee for a close friend. I've told him, with tears in my eyes, that I can tell him things I haven't told anyone else—because he is willing to plumb his depths too. In my experience, this is a very rare experience. We have an intimate relationship of a precious kind.

In clinical settings

The term "transference" is a clinical term and refers to the unconscious transfer of experience from one interpersonal context to another. In transference, we relive past relationships in current situations. They are repeated over and over, and this can be especially true when we are in counseling. For example, we might unconsciously view our therapist as our father or mother and act accordingly. If we had a poor relationship with our fathers or mothers, we can work through those negative feelings with the right therapist who has good boundaries and thus establish trust.

The late Dirck Brown, Ed.D., founder and first executive director for the Post-Adoption Center for Education and Research (PACER), board member of the International Soundex Reunion Registry, former president of the AAC and author of *Clinical Practice in Adoption* said, "I spent about four years in analysis and let me tell you, transference is a wonderful experience—I've seldom felt closer to anyone in my life than to my analyst, John."

Through friendships

I have learned trust through my friend and colleague, Vicky Rockwell. We met at a women's support group and the moment I saw her, I knew I would love her. She was dressed with western-style boot shoes and I thought it so neat that she had the freedom to express who she really was through her choice of clothes.

We were in this group for about two years and one time, when I was extremely depressed and was supposed to be getting ready for Bob to host his entire staff for dinner at our home, I was overwhelmed. I wept as I told the group how I was feeling, and you know what Vicky did? She came over to help me.

She and I live very different lifestyles, but we love each other just as we are. We are no longer in the group but our friendship has continued for more than twenty years. Just the other day we were talking about the mystery and joy of our relationship, and Vicky observed:

> You know, trust is a delicate gift we far too often give when it's not deserved. When we do this, we inevitably get burned, and this restarts the cycle of not being able to trust. Our friendship is unique but not at all surprising. God has taken each of us along very different paths but he has brought us to the same place: his safe presence. I think trust is recognition of the familiar—knowing that we are truly a part of One.

With mentors

I also feel safe with the beautiful older women who have mentored me over the years. At each stage of life and with every move, there has been someone older and wiser than me to help me find the right path.

Rosemary Jensen, founder of The Rafiki Foundation, took me under her wing when I was a new teaching leader in her organization. Even though we don't see each other anymore, the relationship has continued through correspondence. I will never forget one time, right after my birth mother rejected me. Rosemary knew nothing about it, yet in the mail one day I got a note from her that said, "I've been thinking about you. What is going on in your life? How is your writing going?"

In small groups

Bob and I are members of a small group that meets weekly for study and friendship. In the beginning, we all had our best foot forward, but as one person got real, then another, people were freed up to be themselves and share without fear of judgment. It's a guilt-free zone for each person and they have become like family to us.

Risk but beware

It's a reality that not all people are trustworthy, and we need to always keep that in mind, especially when we are needy. Trust is not something we ought to dole out like ice cream on a hot summer day to anyone who comes along. Yet because many of us have emotional vulnerabilities and such a deep need for connection, we sometimes throw all caution to the wind and launch into relationships that tear down instead of build up.

Author Lillian Glass, Ph.D., describes the results of a relationship with such a person. She says:

> A toxic person is someone who seeks to destroy you. A toxic person robs you of your self-esteem and dignity and poisons the essence of who you are. He or she wears down your resistance and thus can make you mentally or physically ill. Toxic people are not life-supporting. They see only the negative in you. Jealous and envious, they are not happy to see you succeed. In fact, they get hostile whenever you do well. Their insecurities and feelings of inadequacy often cause them to sabotage your efforts to lead a happy and productive life.[4]

After we've been burned a few times by toxic relationships, we long for the wisdom and courage to listen to the signals of our bodies and souls. However, more times than we care to remember, we don't recognize or heed the warning signs and find ourselves in relationships with emotionally unhealthy people, in undesirable circumstances, or in commitments for which we have neither the time nor the energy.

Can you pinpoint toxic relationships with anyone in your past or present? Jenny can. She said she had this "friend" who continually pointed out what she thought were Jenny's shortcomings, one of which was an eagerness to get her non-identifying information. The person judged this to be impatience on Jenny's part, simply a wild goose chase to figure out her identity. Jenny says:

> Maybe it was, but she was *judging* me and playing psychoanalyst. When I finally found my birth mother and had a successful experience, she became jealous and told me so in a voice filled with self-pity. Being with her was a little like rubbing up against a porcupine. She was always prickly and I ended up hurt.

Some of us also become enmeshed in toxic situations and relationships when we share too much too soon. We don't put out the necessary "feelers" or "testers" to see how the other person will react to private information. We dive in the deep end of the pool when we haven't even taken beginners' swimming lessons.

Richard Curtis describes such an experience. He says:

> About a year after my reunion with my siblings in Cleveland I was visiting my two half-sisters. While waiting for dinner to be prepared I had an opportunity to spend some time with the middle sister with whom I hadn't had much communication. She asked several questions about my growing-up years as well as my adult life.
>
> Feeling more comfortable with her, I proceeded to reveal personal stories about my experiences in my adoptive home, my broken relationships with spouses, recovery from addictions, and strained relationships with my own children.

She became silent, explaining that my behavior was much like her ex-husband's, with whom she has a volatile relationship.

Oh-oh, Richard, I said to myself. *Too much sharing!*

Since that conversation I've sensed a coolness, a backing away, a judgmental, rejecting attitude toward me. I continue to correspond only with my other sister who has accepted me unconditionally.

Richard's painful experience underscores the truth that trust *must* be earned.

Three characteristics of safe people

Wouldn't it be great if every safe, trustworthy person wore a sign on his or her back that said so? That might qualify as an adoptee fantasy of the highest order! However, there *are* certain characteristics that define safe people, and once we learn them we're much more likely to make wise decisions regarding with whom we share our deepest selves.

They require a two-dimensional relationship

I don't know about you, but I *can't stand* to be in any kind of conversation or relationship in which one person dominates. It absolutely drives me nuts! After the conversation is over, I feel like I've been bound, gagged, and shoved in a corner. These are the kind of people I befriended before I learned about trust. I was a co-dependent, thinking I could rescue them and help them by not sharing my thoughts, but just listening.

That's far from the kind of relationship we're looking for. There has to be a natural give and take, kind of like playing a graceful game of tennis. One shares and then the other responds in a continual, flowing manner.

A key to this kind of relationship is what David Augsburger calls "equal hearing." I love this:

Equal Hearing
I will claim
my right
to be
equally heard.
If I yield
my right to speak,
if I do not claim my time for sharing,
if I do not express what I want in equality,
I am squandering
my privilege of
personhood.
I will respect
your right
to be
equally heard.
You are you.
I want
to hear you.
If I usurp
your right to speak,
if I use up
your time for conversing,
if I do not listen
for what you want in
equality,
I am stifling
your privilege of personhood.[5]

If we've located someone who's not a dominator, but equally as interested in us as he is in himself, we can look for the second characteristic, which is a nonjudgmental attitude.

They're not judgmental

Don't you hate having someone point his or her long, bony finger at you and tell you what you should or shouldn't be doing? In my opinion, this is nothing short of playing God.

I love the saying: "If you can spot it, you got it." It has helped me immensely to learn about the psychological dynamic of projection. My layman's understanding of it is that if someone says something judgmental about me, they're really saying that is how they feel about themselves. Try that next time someone throws a judgmental thought at you. It diffuses your reaction so that you can respond responsibly and not emotionally.

It is my belief that we are all of equal worth and are on a horizontal playing field. One of the most effective ways I can spot people who judge are those who give *unsolicited* advice or counsel. Yes, they may be well-intentioned and even knowledgeable. However, unsolicited counsel is nothing more than a glorified put-down.

Augsburger created a diagram about relationships[6] that I have made myself accountable to for years, and it has literally changed my life. It has helped me sidestep the judgers as well as keep my own attitudes and behavior on track. Notice as you review the diagram that "talking with" is the correct way of relating to others.

	Talking down	
	Blaming	
	Scolding	
	Judging	
	Belittling	
	Instructing	
	Supervising	
Equal Give and take	**Talking with**	**Mutual** Hearing and being heard
	Yielding	
	Ingratiating	
	Groveling	
	Apologizing	
	Placating	
	Talking up	

Once we've weeded out judgmental, self-appointed counselors from our lives, we can put out feelers by observing the reactions of others to our words and feelings. Safe people desire to build up, to reassure us that they care enough about us to invest something of themselves in our lives through words and actions.

They edify through words and actions

Here are some attitudes and actions of people who build up:

- They accept us as we are—they don't try to "fix" us.

- They recognize our potential.

- They believe in us and tell us so.

- They encourage us to "aim high."

- They assure us that they will always be there for us.

- They seek to neutralize our fears.

- They make us laugh.

- They tell the truth when we need to hear it, and they admit their own mistakes readily.

- They give us the freedom to screw up and make mistakes…to be human.

In my book, these basic characteristics are "givens" in finding safe people. Being in their presence is like being in the hollow of a tree—we are safe from the storms of life and safe to tell it like it is.

As we apply what we've learned in this chapter to our lives, we will gradually gain the ability to identity safe people and then develop relationships with them.

Our Choice

To begin searching for safe people, put out feelers, and take a risk.

We must guard our hearts through discernment and simultaneously learn the art of gradual self-disclosure. We need to find a healthy balance between the two, and that will occur as we learn to trust ourselves.

How to begin

- *Make a complete list of your current relationships.* Purchase a binder or set this up on your computer or iPad: make four columns per page. Label four columns like this: *Person, Characteristics of Relationship, Safe or Unsafe?, Action to Be Taken.* See if you can discern if you have clung to unsafe people, and if so, why. Pay special attention to the fourth column.

- *Make a list of all the people you think would be safe.* Who do you admire? If you are in a support group, who do you feel drawn to?

- *Reach out.* After you have identified a new person, invite him or her for coffee. It feels scary to take a risk, but go for it.

Once we've tasted and enjoyed friendships with healthy people, we may look back at old relationships and see how they have fallen short. This may stir up anger, and we'll talk about that next. Oh…that adoptee anger! Will we ever be able to tame it?

Anyone can become angry—that is easy, but to be angry with the right person, to the right degree, at the right time, for the right purpose, and in the right way—this is not easy.

—ARISTOTLE

CHAPTER eight

We *Can* Control Our Anger...Really!

One twenty-something adopted woman stood up in a seminar and asked, "Will it ever go away?"

She was referring to her inability to control her anger, which many adoptees find hugely challenging. It spews from our pores and is communicated through our body language. Yet we may not be self-aware enough to realize what we're communicating.

Our anger can be like a raging lion, seeking to devour everything in its path, while at other times it's like a time bomb, ticking silently, threatening to detonate within our souls. We've all felt it surge through our bodies and minds, possibly escalating into uncontrollable rage. We've felt guilty, victimized, and ashamed for having anger. For many of us, it's been an enemy to be sought out and destroyed at all costs. We've tried:

- taking anger management courses
- counting to ten before exploding
- suppressing it and getting depressed
- venting to a support group.

Many would conclude that the self-help options listed above are all dead-ends. Thus, we might conclude that we were just born filled with rage—it's a personal defect.

You know what, friends, that is a downright lie! We weren't born angry and anger is not a character defect. There is something new we need to learn about anger that will bring it under control. We'll do that here.

There is an extra twist that adoptees must learn about anger, but first, let's look at four reasons we can welcome it.

Four reasons to welcome anger

You may be surprised, as I was, to learn that our job is *not* to eliminate anger, but to *welcome* it as a friend carrying a very important message. "How could it possibly be a friend?" you may be asking. Let's look at why.

It's an innate capacity for preparedness

Anger can be beautiful because it is an innate capacity that is wired into us from conception and something that offers incredible possibilities, if used in the correct way. It alerts our minds and bodies to flee or fight while energizing us for action in response to either physical or psychological danger. It is a state of physical preparedness.

Todd Beamer, a 9/11 American hero, experienced its beauty. Who will ever forget the horrific tragedy of 9/11? It is burned into our memories forever. Can you imagine how Todd felt when he learned that the plane he was flying in was going to be turned into a missile that would destroy the White House? He must have been terrified in a way that is unimaginable for most of us. He was staring death straight in the face.

Todd told GTE telephone supervisor, Lisa Jefferson, by cell phone that he and fellow passengers Jeremy Glick and Thomas Burnett, Jr had decided they would not be pawns in the hijackers' wicked plot. The innate physiological component of anger propelled them out of their seats and helped them rally other passengers to take action.

Armed with nothing but their own courage and a plastic butter knife from their airplane breakfast, Todd Beamer rallied his fellow passengers: "Are you ready? Let's roll." The passengers attacked the terrorists, took over the plane, and forced it to crash outside of Pittsburgh, killing every person on board but undoubtedly saving many other lives.

It's not wrong

For those of us with a faith-based belief system, we might be misled by pontificating preachers who only give half-truths about anger. We don't want to do wrong, so we suppress it. That is what I did for years. I am reminded of these words: "Go ahead and be angry. You do well to be angry—but don't use your anger as fuel for revenge. And don't stay angry. Don't go to bed angry."[1]

Todd Beamer displayed healthy anger. What was the first thing he did? He humbled himself, called 9-1-1, and prayed with the operator. He knew he had a vital, life-giving mission to accomplish before he left planet Earth.

It's a secondary emotion

Another aspect of anger is that it's a secondary emotion. That means that there is a trigger that produces what is called a primary emotion. After the primary emotion, such as fear, is triggered, the secondary emotion, which is anger, kicks in. I like to think of the primary emotion as a wound and the secondary emotion as a scab over the wound. The wound has to occur *before* the scab forms. Thus, anger is secondary.

The triggering event for Todd Beamer was the news that not only was he facing death, but possibly so were the President, government officials, and employees at the US Capitol. Terror would likely have been the primary emotion in response to the pain. And then anger.

If we could talk to Todd today, I bet he would tell us how thankful he is that he was so wonderfully wired. Without that physiological response to danger, he would have sat paralyzed in his seat and the US would have been further devastated.

It might be a sign we are coming to life

A therapist friend of mine once said that she believes anger is like a sacrament—something sacred that must be revered and something that can give life. Because of this belief she asks her clients to demonstrate their anger in a way that is unique and safe.

One client brought in a beautiful vase that belonged to her late mother (no...not the one that held her ashes!), and during one session in the therapist's office she smashed it to smithereens while shouting all the things she was angry at her mother about. Afterward there was release and freedom. She was moving out of numbness to experiencing a fuller spectrum of her emotions, and she celebrated with her therapist.

Triggers for primary emotions

As we reflect on these aspects of anger, we can conclude that anger, if handled correctly, has the potential for being a good thing. As adoptees, I believe it is important for us to know the common triggers for our primary emotions so we will understand the source of our anger and discover healthy ways to manage it.

Being sent away by our birth mothers

An interesting article about adoptee anger is written by a birth mother named Carol Komissaroff. She says:

> What are adoptees angry about? Lots of things. They're angry with people like me because we gave them away. They need an explanation and an apology. Of course they can't get one because we're nowhere to be found, which frustrates them and makes them mad as hell. Some are also angry because we sent them away from their 'kind,' abandoning them to an environment in which they suffer a chronic, cumulative, vast feeling of unacceptability. The pain, helplessness, and frustration caused by that sort of thing can make a person very mad.[2]

Dirck Brown says:

> I spent a year in analysis before I even mentioned that I was adopted, and even then I was very tentative about talking about it. My analyst commented when I began to talk about it that I seemed to be furious and that what he sensed I really wanted to do was strangle my birth mother!

Kim Norman says that her blood didn't begin to boil until she began looking into the impact of adoption on her relationship problems. It was then that her feelings polarized about adoption.

She concluded that adoption is the worst thing a birth mother can do to a child:

> My birth mother wasn't trying to care for me—she simply decided the easy way out was to give me up when I was one month old. The question I ask is, 'What attempts did she really make in order to keep me?'

Being treated like second-class citizens

Another common trigger is being treated like a second-class citizen, for many reasons.

As this book is penned, many adoptees in the US can't have access to their original birth certificates. Why is this important? It is important because it proves:

- We are real people.
- We had a real birth.
- We had a mother who gave us birth.
- We were at a real hospital.

Kim Norman is still very angry about one aspect of being adopted—the fact that she feels like a second-class citizen legally:

> I am angry that I am not legally entitled to my *true* birth certificate! The information represented on that piece of paper is about *me*, yet I can't have a copy. I am angry at the way the system is—that there wasn't someone present thirty-two years ago raising these types of questions when I was adopted.

There are many ways that adoptees report feeling second class. Here are a few:

- For the foster child who ages out of the system, no matter what country, with nothing but the shirt on her back, she feels incredibly second class, if that. She's angry at people who use words like "forever" in regard to "forever families." To her, "forever" is like the "f word." As she tries to make her way in the world, society often treats her as a loser child.

- The media, at least in the US, always reports that if someone did something bad, he was "the adopted son of _____," some famous person.

- What about adoptees who have a different skin color than their parents? Do they not feel second class when others ask who their real family is?

- How about racism? Comments like, "Send her back to her own country where they grow coconuts."

- How about international adoptees who are sent to their new homes with only a certificate of abandonment? Ouch.

Feeling unworthy of anything good

Another injustice is not feeling free to ask for what we need. Do you ever find yourself shrinking back when someone offers you a choice between two gifts—one more appealing to you than the other? Perhaps the person offers you the choice between a silk or burlap scarf. She says, "Go ahead, take the *silk* scarf," and you say, "Oh, that's okay. The burlap one will be fine."

I do that all the time! I don't feel like I'm entitled to ask for the silk scarf (what I need and love). Why is that? Is it because I don't feel worthy enough to have anything good?

Connie Dawson says that not feeling entitled to ask for or receive what we need as human beings—unconditional love and connection—naturally leads us to feeling angry. She says, "Hurt? 'You bet I've been hurt and of course I am angry' is what my 'inside baby' wants to say—stomping her foot to claim her entitlement to her feelings."

Cheri Freeman says that she lived a nightmarish childhood with a father who was mentally ill and full of rage. When her parents eventually divorced when she was seventeen, she *finally* expressed some of her pent-up anger toward her adoptive father. The next morning, he showed up at the courthouse and terminated his parental rights and responsibilities. "Of course, he couldn't have done that unless her new stepfather was willing to adopt me, but I felt like I'd been rejected forever and banned from the family for expressing anger."

What *will* tame our anger?

Forgive me if you already know this and it seems simplistic. For me, it has been a game changer.

There are two kinds of anger—misplaced and healthy. Misplaced anger often is directed at our adoptive or foster moms, as we are furious with our birth mothers for disappearing from our presence, even if just in the parenting role, as in open adoption.

We've already discussed healthy anger and its purpose that has been innately wired into us.

I don't know about you, but I clumped all anger together—misplaced and healthy. I didn't know the difference and concluded that "I'm an angry person."

There's the lie I believed for most of my life. I was ashamed of my anger and wondered if there was something wrong with me because it was so intense.

We need to identify and then work through misplaced anger and get rid of it. As we work hard, the power of the misplaced anger will slowly fade. My husband says of me, "You're not so angry anymore."

We need to find appropriate ways to express anger that are not destructive to ourselves or others. Here are several to get us started.

Remain responsible through affirmations

I don't know about you, but when I get angry my natural response is to run away. I did this as a child and I am embarrassed to say I have done it as a grown, married woman. There have been many nights when I've packed my bag and called my favorite inn in Michigan for a reservation. The trouble is that I took the pain with me. Geographical solutions don't work.

We can choose to remain responsible. I am learning to say to myself, *Sherrie, you are a grown woman with a family who loves you dearly. You would only be hurting them and yourself if you made this rash decision to pack up and leave.*

Pause and evaluate

It is important to remember that there is a fleeting second between primary and secondary emotions. That fleeting second provides us with a choice. Will we react impulsively or respond responsibly? We're not victims of anger. We have a choice about how to behave!

Cheri Freeman is trying to learn to respond in the right way by backing off for a "time-out" before sharing angry feelings with anyone. "I can show irritation and frustration easily enough, but anger and fear are harder for me to share maturely."

Refuse to retaliate

If we blame others for our emotional pain, we give *them* power over what we think, feel, say, and do. Blaming statements such as "They are doing it to me," or "She makes me so angry," reveal a victim's mind-set. Nobody can *make* us angry. In any situation we have the power to identify our primary emotion and choose how we will respond in a way that preserves our dignity and safety.

It helps me tremendously to recall this verse, "Don't insist on getting even; that's not for you to do. 'I'll do the judging,' says God. 'I'll take care of it.'"[3]

How much better to have a higher court deal with rejecting/cruel people? This verse says it aptly: "But how is it to your credit if you receive a beating for doing wrong and endure it? But if you suffer for doing good and you endure it, this is commendable before God."[4]

Welcome healthy anger

For many of us, anger has turned inward and become depression. We may have been the good little adoptee and suppressed it. We are shut down. But when we begin to *feel* angry, it can be a sign that we're coming to life!

The late Dirck Brown, when confronted by his analyst about his anger, said, "I was able to begin to feel my deep, deep anger and resentment over being rejected, abandoned—that Gretchen (my birth mother) did not want me and perhaps didn't want to have me from the very beginning."

Connie Dawson says that when she and her husband separated, she couldn't hold back.

> Oh, I was still 'nice', but I'd never felt anger as I felt it then. I've done a lot of rage work in therapy. I still get angry, but most of the original abandonment anger at being 'put out' as a baby has receded. Now when I'm angry I take it as a signal that there is a *current* problem to solve. I think of all those years I couldn't afford to express my anger for fear I'd be sent away, abandoned again. What a waste of good time.

And so what is the choice we need to make at this juncture?

Our Choice

To identify and process misplaced anger.

How to begin

- *Make an anger chart.* Beginning as far back as you can remember, list all the things you have felt angry about. Then go back over the list and see if you can identify the primary emotion (unmet need) beneath the anger. Ask yourself: "What was the predominant injury?"

- *List the primary people in your life with whom you have anger issues.* Then, write *Misplaced anger* or *Healthy anger* after each person.

- *Search for answers that will satisfy you about anger.* Theologians, great writers, ordinary people.

- *Write a letter TO and FROM your birth mother.* Use an online feelings chart as well as an online thesaurus to amplify your descriptions (www.csefel.uiuc.edu is a good place to begin). Experts say this is the best way for adoptees to surface repressed emotions.

- *Identify some untrue beliefs about yourself and anger and then counter them with a truthful affirmation.* For example, "I'm just an angry person" versus "I am a precious person."

As we identify misplaced anger and the work involved to move past it, certainly the days will be painful...but productive. Keep pressing on!

That which does not kill us makes us stronger.

—FRIEDRICH NIETZSCHE

CHAPTER nine

We Can Get Unstuck from Our Painful Past

Avoid the pain! Avoid it at all costs. After all, isn't life filled with enough of it? Whether from aging out of the system, being abandoned on an orphanage step as a baby, contacting a rejecting birth relative, being the brunt of racism, well-meaning words that cause pain from religious folk, having no birth history, or having a birth history you'd never choose, or divorcing your incredible spouse because you're terrified of intimacy…our natural tendency is to run.

Avoidance techniques for adoption-related pain don't seem to differ much from those that people use in response to other painful situations in life. Adopted or not, many of us resort to food, sex, relationship obsession, alcohol, drugs, fanatical religion, suicide, or extramarital affairs…and the list goes on.

Ways we get stuck

As I've interviewed hundreds of adoptees, I've discovered that we use "all of the above" and more—but that four styles are particularly prevalent.

Pretend we're happy

Compartmentalizing the pain. Throwing ourselves into mindless activity. Acting and saying everything is fine when it isn't. Holding back tears. Faking a smile. These are just a few of the ways we numb ourselves.

Kenny Tucker, adoption activist, says that he just numbs out emotionally from tough issues so that he can properly digest them later in smaller chunks.

Cheri Freeman says that when simple denial doesn't work, she turns to outright disassociation. If she can't talk herself out of feeling bad she buries herself in a book or a series of books or does some marathon sleeping. She knows the pain will still be there when she finishes the last book or wakes up, but at least by then it might be blunted.

Joy Budensiek, author of *Reconnected—To My Bellybutton*, says:

> When something is painful to me, I mentally put it in a box, tie it up tight, and put it on a high shelf in my mind, not to be taken down until the edge of the pain is gone. Or, I mentally shut a door, not to be opened until it is safe. Disassociation may have its "down sides," but it may also keep me from falling apart.

We may have been numbing ourselves since early childhood; for many of us it's become a "survival skill." However, the unfortunate result is that we don't develop the capacity to fully enter into life and also *enjoy* the present moment. We're somewhere else instead. The lights are on but nobody's home.

Compulsive overeating

Another behavior used to run from our feelings is compulsive overeating. When I was attending a support group years ago someone said, "Food is the number-one addiction." That statement rang true because food is something we *need* in order to live. We can't eliminate it from our lives like an alcoholic can eliminate alcohol. Food is always there, staring us in the face.

Richard Curtis says that whenever he tells his adoption story he always includes his obsession with food.

It is an integral part of my story because it overshadows all my other means of escaping from pain, including addiction to alcohol. As a little kid, as far back as I can remember, I sought food for comfort in dealing with sadness, fear, loneliness, and other painful feelings I couldn't identify. Food became my friend, my solace, and my comforter.

Compulsive overeating, however, is a silent partner that is overlooked by society and actually encouraged by well-meaning friends and family members. As an adult the cycle of bingeing on food and purging through exercise increased my excess weight, and I kept the bingeing and purging a secret. My behavior destroyed my self-esteem and physical and spiritual well-being. No diets or pills were able to reverse the cycle of eating that was spinning out of control and leading to suicidal tendencies.

Today, after much counseling, even though I have enjoyed almost ten years of sobriety from alcohol, the addiction to food continues to raise its ugly head from time to time—most recently resulting in a hospital stay for a digestive disorder.

Phyllis-Anne Munro says she suppressed painful feelings through overeating. Sad to say, overeating was the only bond with her adoptive mother, since her mother equated food with love.

Compulsive eating not only numbs the pain, it makes the scales go up while our emotional health goes down…down…down.

Drug addictions

Another means of escape is drugs, whether legal or illegal, that come in a variety of forms and shapes. While they *temporarily* relieve pain, when misused to run from our feelings they can easily become addictive. Our bodies and minds crave more and more, and we'll go to almost any length to get it.

Lori says:

> I was a drug addict for twenty-three years. This was my way of keeping the painful belief away that "nobody loves me." I started smoking pot when I was eleven. Over the course of time, I've tried every drug known to mankind except heroin—the only smart decision I made at the time. I knew that if I tried it I would love it and it would kill me.

Courtney asked her psychiatrist to give her something for stress, believing that she just couldn't cope with life any longer. She just wanted something to "take the edge off." Her physician prescribed an anti-anxiety drug called Ativan. It worked wonders at first, but then its effectiveness began to wear off and Courtney rationalized taking more and more of the drug. Before long she was in a psychiatric ward of a hospital.

Currently, in the US, marijuana is being legalized. You can even buy marijuana-laced brownies.

Without a doubt, doing drugs is not the answer to our problems.

Workaholism

Workaholism is just as insidious as drug abuse. If we are pleaser-type adoptees, we may develop this from childhood. When I meet an adoptive parent who raves about his child's achievements, a huge red flag goes up for me.

Like overeating, workaholism is another "acceptable addiction" in nearly every society. Bring the briefcase home every night. Work late. Miss meals. Go into the office early. Climb, climb, climb that corporate ladder. Reach the top. How exhilarating! Success is the goal, and if we obtain it, surely we won't have any problems…really?

Sharon says:

When I was only fifteen, I decided that I would rather work than go to school. I reasoned that the money I would earn would buy my freedom from having to depend on *anyone* for *anything*; I could take care of myself if I had the money.

I worked as much as possible and became wildly successful, which gave me a false sense of safety, control, and self-esteem. By the time I was twenty, I was a fully-fledged workaholic. I couldn't stop overworking. I thought it was the only way for me to have value in my own eyes as well as in the eyes of others.

When my company was taken over and I was transferred out of the area that I had created, I wanted to die because work was all that was holding me up. I finally sought counseling. Thanks to counseling, prayer, and letting myself finally grieve my early losses, I am much better now, although I know it would be very easy to slip into the old patterns.

Some of us might feel caught in an inescapable addiction right now. We've tried everything conceivable, yet nothing has worked. Is there any solution? Any hope? You bet!

Another way to think about pain

Let me share another way to think about pain through a story about a man named Paul who had some kind of physical ailment that he called his "thorn in the flesh." No one is really sure what it was, but it was so painful that he prayed to have it taken away. Three times he pleaded, but each time the answer was no.

In the years that followed, Paul's "thorn" remained, yet in the process he learned a valuable lesson—rewards come as we move *through* pain and suffering. Paul began to experience a certain kind of strength that came in the midst of weakness and powerlessness. He received profound wisdom about life and death that those new to suffering couldn't possibly comprehend. He even got to the point of being thankful for the pain because he knew that pain ushered him into the very place where he would be ready to receive these wonderful character qualities. Paul learned to welcome pain as a holy guest in disguise. Ultimately, Paul became the person he was created to be simply because he learned to embrace his pain instead of running from it.[1]

"*Embrace* it?" you may be muttering under your breath. "Sherrie, you're getting a little far out. That sounds like a bunch of psychobabble. And anyway, how could I possibly *welcome* pain? That sounds pretty nuts, actually."

I hear you. But I have discovered, as have many of my fellow adoptees, emotional and spiritual riches as we've allowed ourselves to be broken—body, soul, and spirit. As we've finally allowed ourselves to feel the anguish of loss, the distress of mixed feelings, the agony of loneliness, the throes of anger, we have experienced divine grace to endure, to be patient, to surrender our wills upward in all humility. As a result of this excruciating process, we have reaped sweet rewards: joy instead of depression; love for others instead of sick self-absorption; self-control instead of uncontrollable addictions to food, alcohol, and people; contentment and security instead of anxiety; courage instead of panic; deep wisdom instead of shallow, numbed-out living; and for those with a religious faith, knowing God and ourselves better.

I remember when I was suffering from my second clinical depression. I was an outpatient at Methodist Hospital in Indianapolis, which meant I came home every night. I couldn't do anything for myself. I could barely talk intelligibly. Patients and some nurses at the hospital felt sorry for me and spoke for me. I had to drop out of my graduate program when I was one of ten who had been handpicked. I couldn't cook a meal. I couldn't drive the car. I was terrified of my beloved psychiatrist who spent an hour a day in therapy with me. I was totally broken...again.

I know without a doubt that pain can be redeemed for those who believe. Derek Jeske, who experienced a transracial adoption, has found this to be true. He says, "I have come to embrace pain because I have the knowledge and understanding that I can teach others to accept who they are regardless of where they come from or who their parents are."

It has always been helpful for me when considering the topic of pain to recall a story about a little boy who was watching a cecropia moth break away from its cocoon. The moth's struggle to be free seemed excruciatingly slow to the little boy, so in his pity for the moth he decided to give it some help by widening the cocoon's opening and making it easier to escape.

The boy watched with anticipation as the moth freed itself from the cocoon. He couldn't wait for the wings to fill out so it could fly.

But something was wrong. Instead of the wings becoming strong, they remained shriveled. What the little boy didn't realize was that *struggle is essential* in developing a good muscle system that can pump blood into the moth's wings. The moth was crippled forever because the boy removed the pressures.[2]

So it will be for us if we choose to run from our pain. We'll be removing the struggle needed to develop healthy wings so that we can fly away from our painful pasts. And so, what is a life-transforming choice in regard to the pain we may be avoiding in association with being adopted?

Our Choice

To accept our painful past as preparation for our life purpose and passion.

How to begin

- *Admit you've done your best* to avoid the repercussions of a painful past.

- *Make a list of the ways that your life has spun out of control through running from pain.* Be brutally honest. No one else gets to see the list, so don't hold back. Specifically identify your own patterns.

- *Reframe your past pain.* Ask yourself, "What is the most painful thing that has ever happened to me?" Then, realize that our greatest pains can become springboards to our life purpose and calling.

- *Draw two templates (two large squares side-by-side).* On the left template, put words that describe your painful past as well as your reactions to the pain. That is what you've lived in for a lifetime. But now there's another template set beside it that has nothing written on it. Write how this pain might become a springboard for personal, professional, relational, and spiritual growth.

- *Cultivate a thankful spirit.* This will be sacrificial…it won't be natural or come easy. However, as you begin to see your painful past as part of the grand design for your life, thankfulness will bring healing to places in your heart you're not even aware of. Whispering "thank you" is kind of like planting a flower seed in a Dixie cup. You plant the seed well into the dirt, set it on the window ledge for light, and water it diligently for days. All you can see is dirt. Plain dirt. How discouraging! But then you discover one morning that a little green sprout has popped up through the dirt, and you realize that it was growing and thriving all along—you just couldn't see it. That's the way it is when we give thanks—not for the pain itself, not for the circumstances, but for the *transformation* that is going on in the secret places of our hearts. Thankfulness waters your soul.

While we're waiting for that little seed to grow, however, we may experience feelings of loss at a new level. Let's explore that next.

Our echoes roll from soul to soul, and grow forever and forever.

— LORD ALFRED TENNYSON, *THE PRINCESS*

CHAPTER **ten**

Many of Us Experience Echoes of Loss

Imagine yourself standing on a cliff at the Grand Canyon. You cup your hands to your mouth and yell something into the wide open cavern. Within seconds you can hear your words echo…echo…echo…until all is silent again.

It's a wondrous experience for tourists at the Grand Canyon but not so for adoptees who hear different kinds of echoes. What if the words yelled down the Grand Canyons of our souls were "I'm gone forever…forever…forever. You are alone…you are alone…you are alone"?

Well, it isn't a "what if" situation. Those words *were* yelled down the canyons of our adoptee hearts when we lost our birth parents either at birth or later in life. And throughout life, we hear the same echoes…in different circumstances, different volumes, and different relationships. The echoes might diminish to almost a whisper but they aren't completely quieted until this life is over.

The echoes we hear

From this core message of loss other messages emerge. While we may not attribute them to our adoption experience, it may be a significant contributor.

Absence equals abandonment

It seems a common theme among adoptees that if we can't literally see somebody we love, we conclude that we are abandoned.

A few years ago my husband and I traveled to Chicago to see a play. The next morning I went for a walk before leaving while Bob made some business calls. After finishing my walk and returning to the hotel room, the door to our room was locked. I knocked and knocked, expecting Bob to swing it wide open, but no one answered. I knocked again, harder, but still no answer.

My heart was pounding as I quickly scanned the hall. There was a maid across the hallway who reluctantly agreed to open the door. When she opened it I saw the unmade bed and used towels in the bathroom, but no Bob. No suitcases. No note explaining why he wasn't there. Nothing!

I ran down to the elevator thinking, *Maybe he wants a divorce and just decided to leave. After all, I've been far from the perfect wife and I sure wouldn't blame him if he did.*

Upon entering the lobby and looking out into the car entrance, there was Bob, *casually* loading our bags in the trunk of the car. He looked so innocent that I wanted to wring his neck!

"Why did you leave without a note or *something*?" I demanded.

"Honey, I just thought I'd save us some time and that you'd be glad we're ready to go," he answered calmly.

I sobbed as we "discussed" the incident on the way home and at one point I admitted, "I thought you left me."

There was that echo again. My husband's unexplained and temporary absence translated to my adoptee heart as abandonment.

Sue has had similar experiences. She says one time her teenage daughter flew overseas for a summer of volunteer work and she thought they were going to have to call in the Emergency Room swat team for her. As the plane departed, Sue described big, gulping sobs that lasted for a long time. She felt like she was saying goodbye to her daughter forever.

Phyllis-Anne Munro says that she has always feared that loved ones won't return, and as a result has made a pact with them to call when they arrive at their destinations. This somewhat soothes her fears.

Five-year-old Katy Puckett seems to always have a crisis when her mom leaves to go anywhere without her. Her mom, Robbin says, "It's becoming worse the older she gets; the only thing she can explain to me is that she 'worries that I won't be back.'"

Being alone is scary

Another echo involves being alone. Lori says she now knows she has suffered from "abandonment phobia" all her life, and that is why she hates to be alone. After failed marriages she realized she was willing to stay in bad relationships just to be with someone. "I needed people so bad that I would go to hell and back to keep from losing them, even when they were clearly not good for me."

Another echo makes us restless and discontent in relationships and responsibilities.

Don't tie me down

For many of us, our hearts are in a perpetual searching mode. We're looking for something, but we're not sure what. Thus, our contentment and commitment levels fluctuate, like a roller coaster.

Paul says that if it wasn't for his wife and kids, he'd be a mountain man. There he wouldn't have any responsibility except for himself. Some days he feels like running away, but knows he can't, out of love for his family.

Renee has been through three marriages, but after working through adoption-related issues, she is in a "committed relationship."

This tendency toward restlessness has also seeped into her career life. Even though she's always had a career, she changed jobs ten times between the ages of twenty-two and thirty-seven. She says she's still looking for one that "sticks."

Richard Curtis says that by grace he began to realize in his previous three failed marriages that he had not allowed his wives to know the *real* Richard. Instead he hid behind the mask of "nice guy." He wouldn't allow himself to fully commit in any relationship without having "one foot out the door."

Conform, achieve, and be perfect

Another message from the echo involves conformity, overachievement, and perfectionism. If we're perfect and if we adapt to what other people expect, we won't have to experience any more abandonment, right?

Dr. Reverend Richard Gilbert says that he has needed to excel through work and socialization. He has sought approval and, in countless ways, tried to prove to the world (and himself) that his birth parents made a bad decision.

Sue says she tried so hard as a kid to succeed through overachievement, but to no avail. Nobody knew she had what is now called attention deficit hyperactivity disorder (ADHD). All she ever heard was that she wasn't achieving up to potential and that she needed to try harder. "If I had tried any harder I would have ground myself into dust. That still makes me sad to think about. Very little that I did was seen as really, really good."

Kim Norman says she has always been an overachiever and that her supergirl efforts were driven by the hope that if she excelled, her parents would *truly* love her, even though in reality, they already did. Her ability to receive their love was damaged and so they could never express how much they loved her *enough* to soothe her adoptee heart.

"Overachieving? Yes, of course," says Connie Dawson. "It's how I could deserve to be cared for, because my parents loved pointing to me as successful to prove they were successful. I call it [overachieving] 'earning my keep.'"

Don't get too close

One of the strongest messages that comes from that core experience of loss is a fear of intimacy. Drs. Patrick Thomas Malone and Thomas Patrick Malone define intimacy this way:

> Intimacy is derived from the Latin *intima*, meaning "inner" or "innermost." Your inside being is the real you, the you that only you can know. The problem is that you can know it only when you are being intimate with something or someone outside yourself.[1]

Connie Dawson responds, "Surely you jest! If I don't know myself, how can I be intimate with you? If I can't trust you, how can I afford to disclose anything that might make you leave me?"

Renee says she was the classic teen chameleon, adapting her personality to fit in with whatever crowd she was running with. As far as achieving, she got straight As, was in the honor society and student government, on yearbook staff, pom pom (captain!), and tennis team. "Should I go on?" she says, "Of course I always felt that if anyone knew the 'real me' they wouldn't have chosen me to do those things."

Rose says she wants her friends to like her best, but if they really knew her, they wouldn't. She is critical of her husband, accusing him of not being intimate, but she wonders if the core problem is hers. "With sexual intimacy, I can say that the 'real thing' has never happened because I just can't commit my body to another person—it is not an enjoyable part of my life."

Kasey Hamner says that not only does she expect herself to be perfect, but also her partner. When he's not, she struggles with feelings of hatred and disgust. However, she keeps working on her reactions and is growing each day, even though it still seems really scary to her.

Phyllis-Anne Munro admits that in college a friend constantly confronted her about her inability to be real in front of others. Her fear of rejection was so huge that she allowed hardly anyone to see her pain. "I didn't even know how much pain I was in and how fearful I was until I started going to therapy," Phyllis-Anne confesses.

Trish DePew says:

I can't handle the closeness others might desire. I have friends but not many close friends because of the intimacy it takes. I don't think they would like me if they really knew me. If a friend and I have a disagreement, I will turn off my feelings and close down our friendship rather than face whatever is wrong between us.

I'll never get out of this pit

Many of us have struggled with depression. All people do at one time or another in life, but for adoptees it seems to be more prevalent. In a research article, a group of adoptees was interviewed and compared to a control group in order to determine the psychosocial well-being of the adoptees. Adoptees in the sample expressed more depression than their peers, and exceeded the norm for clinical depression by 30 percent. Despite the higher incidence of clinical depression among adoptees, they were no more likely to have sought counseling for depression than those in the control group.[2]

Jody Moreen of Naperville, Illinois, wife, mother of three sons, adoption triad support group facilitator, and editor of *Adoption Blessings* newsletter, says that her depression first showed up when she was a junior in college and her father decided to take early retirement and move south with her mom. As clinical depression gradually set in, she lost her appetite, found life joyless despite her faithful friends and boyfriend, and couldn't concentrate on schoolwork, which led to dropping out for a term. During this crisis time her parents were very concerned and sought medical and psychological services for her.

This pattern of depression repeated a couple of times with geographical moves. The loss of family, friends, familiarity, and security that came with these moves shook Jody's emotional foundation "like an earthquake."

Jan says:

I believe I am suffering from depression right now. I've taken the evaluation questionnaire and five or six symptoms are present. I believe it started years ago. In fact, I believe it may have begun as a child. I remember one instance at school and even the color of dress I was wearing. I was walking down the hall and thinking, "I just can't take it any more—all this stuff is just too much".

Kasey Hamner says she still struggles with depression. Looking at her life on paper is like looking at a dream. Great job. Good income. Devoted boyfriends. Two homes. Good health. Yet still…periods of hopelessness and fear that all she holds dear will be lost.

These are just a few of the messages the core echo brings. Perhaps you can add some of your own…or maybe you aren't aware of any.

Why some adoptees claim no painful repercussions

I wonder why there is such a contrast in our reactions to loss. I sat next to an adopted woman at a dinner last week. Did she have any painful thoughts? No. Did she feel sad that she was given up? No. Did she wish she had searched for her origins earlier, since she found her mother's tombstone at the end of her search? No. Adoptees I've spoken with who don't hear the echoes so common to many of us may have had different childhood experiences, or just different coping mechanisms. Then again, many of them aren't ready to awaken from the long adoptee sleep.

Highly effective parenting

Some attribute excellent parenting to not feeling repercussions. Greg Berger, the graphic artist who created the special edition adoption postal stamp, says, "*Not once* in my life did I consider myself abandoned, even in my simplistic thinking as a young child. This I attribute directly to my adoptive parents."

Melinda Faust, adopted at four months of age from Seoul, South Korea, and a student at Miami University in Ohio, says that adoption has always been such a blessing in her life and never a burden. She's never felt abandoned, or that her biological family didn't love her, or that she's alone. She attributes this to both sets of parents—her adoptive parents, through their incredible openness and love, and her birth family, whom she believes made the ultimate sacrifice for her good. "Only blessings and love resulted from my adoption, and it feels wonderful to be so blessed," Melinda says.

Perseverance

Kimberly Steiner says:

> Through my experience of an international adoption (Korean into a Caucasian family) I've been able to experience and learn about minorities, discrimination, and what it's like to persevere. I've been strengthened through my adoption experience.
>
> At the same time, I've dealt with more experiences than what I feel a "normal" person would go through. I've been dealt a loss that I believe is unique to adoptees. On the other hand, I know that as a result I have worked that much harder to get through these issues. The knowledge I have gained will continue to help me become a more diverse and open person, with much depth. In that regard, I'm so thankful for my adoption; it has brought out my most beautiful qualities and has strengthened me.

Repression

Another reason we may not hear echoes is that we are masters at repression. Dr. Arthur Janov says:

Primal pains arise not only from lack of love but from those epiphanic moments or scenes when a child realizes he is not loved and will not be. They arise when he is shaken for a brief moment by the understanding that he cannot be what he is and be loved, for that moment and for other moments of equally monumental hopelessness.

He then struggles with all his heart to be what parents want him to be. He puts away the pain, or rather it is automatically put away from him by our miraculous system of repression. The repression effectively produces two selves at war with each other: the real self, loaded with needs and pain; and the unreal self, the self out of touch with the other self that was still able to deal with the outside world. The function of the unreal self is to keep the real self from showing its face. Its role is to make the body perform despite the turmoil going on below. The best way to do this, it seems, is for the unreal self to remain ignorant of its own history.[3]

These speculations as to why some of us don't experience primal feelings of loss aren't definitive, but nevertheless, they are good food for thought. For the rest of us who do experience repercussions resulting from adoption loss, we can take heart: the echoes will become fainter and fainter as time goes by if we choose to process them in a healthy manner.

Our Choice

To identify repercussions from adoption loss and grieve them.

For those of us who feel the loss, the only path toward peace and health is to grieve, for grief is to the soul as a fever is to the body. Grief is our heart's way of healing itself. We need to grieve for the life that might have been had we not been adopted. Grieve for the parents we may never lay eyes on. Grieve for the family structure and love we may have missed in our birth families. Grieve for the arms that might have held us. Grieve for the culture we might have known. Grieve over our struggle to be real and intimate with others. Grieve for pushing ourselves to the hilt. Grieve for years wasted on perfectionism.

How to begin

- *Read some good books on the grieving process.* Personally, I like materials by Dr. Henry Cloud, Steve Arterburn, and New Life Resources.

- *Get psychiatric help.* If you are unable to keep from spiraling downward with depression, have your General Practitioner write a referral for you to a respected psychiatrist in your region. Even though your GP is good, he doesn't have the specialized training for this. Psychiatrists are medical physicians who specialize in brain chemistry and imbalances. I have seen so many people messed up by seeking expertise from other kinds of physicians who are not qualified to diagnose or treat clinical depression. And remember as we seek help to have no shame. It's not a defect in character, but in chemistry.

Well, we've hit rock bottom in our process of our transformation process, and the only way now is up!

As you allow yourself to really feel emotions, you will need to be in the presence of growing fellow adoptees. We'll talk about that next.

Friendship makes prosperity brighter, while it lightens adversity by sharing its grief and anxieties.

—CICERO

CHAPTER eleven

An Hour with a Fellow Adoptee Is Better than Weeks of Therapy

I'll never forget sitting next to an adoptive mom at an adoption carnival where I was speaking. At the end of the day the time came for the children and teens to come on stage to show the parents an adoption art project they had been working on.

When all the kids were in place, one of the leaders yelled over the microphone, "Who's adopted here?"

Everyone's hands flew up and squeals of delight burst forth from the little ones. "Me!" they yelled in unison.

The mom leaned over to me and said, "I've *never* seen that expression on my daughter's face. Look at her! When she yelled 'me,' her face absolutely glowed!"

Something unique happened within her daughter that day. What was it? Was it the excitement of being with kids the same age? Was it a sense of pride about her art project or a love of the spotlight?

I don't think so. I believe it was because she had been given a beautiful gift that was brand new to her—the gift of fellow adoptees. It's a gift adoptive parents can't give. A gift birth parents can't give. A gift adoption and mental health professionals can't give. Only other adoptees can give it to one another. It is a precious commodity!

Something extraordinary happens when adoptees connect with one another. You can't touch it. You can't see it. You can't feel it. But among the adoptees, a sense of connection occurs that is just as real as the clouds in the sky. There is an unspoken bond. A feeling of camaraderie. A reassurance of being understood. A sense of belonging.

It wasn't until I was forty-five that I met my first adoptee friend. From the moment we had our first lunch together, we became fast friends. We would sit for hours at our favorite little tearoom, sip spiced tea, and talk about adoption. It was wonderful. As we spent time together and opened our hearts, we discovered that even though the circumstances of our adoptions and adoptive homes were different, common threads united us in almost every sphere of our lives.

I learned that having an adoptee as a friend is a blessing par excellence. When I didn't have one, I didn't know what I was missing. It was like growing up never having tasted triple-chocolate cake!

If we *do* have an adoptee friend, then we realize that he or she is a true blessing, sent our way to strengthen, encourage, and validate all that we are, all that we were, and all that we have yet to become.

Why we love to be together

Why do adoptees enjoy being together so much? What creates that special bond?

This may be difficult for the non-adopted person to understand, but there is something almost mystical that happens when two or more adoptees gather together. Why? Because we are like *family*.

We are like family

Richard Curtis says that we share a common bond that unites us across all ages, genders, races, and religions, bringing understanding that we are there for one another as we seek truth and openness in adoption.

Seven-year-old Maggie Backiewicz says, "My friends are my friends! But, with my adopted friends, it seems like we're related in some way."

Penny Callan Partridge remembers how important it was to her to know that there was a fellow adoptee in her elementary school class:

Even though he and I never talked about being adopted, there was comfort in knowing I was not alone. Then there was my excitement when I was on my way to my first adoption meeting in New York City in 1972. My excitement was actually focused on seeing what other adoptees were going to look like! Soon after that, another adopted woman and I started Adoption Forum in Philadelphia—primarily so we wouldn't have to go all the way to New York to talk with other adoptees.

Now, almost thirty years later, two of Penny's closest friends are adopted women, and her two closest male friends are adopted men. "The adopted are certainly 'my people,'" Penny says, "the way others might identify with an ethnic group. I believe that connecting with other adopted people has been just as important to me as finding my birth relatives. I cannot imagine my life without both."

Kim Norman says that fellow adoptees tend to be some of the most compassionate and understanding people she has ever met and that she feels "a special kinship" with them.

Jody Moreen says that knowing other adoptees has created a wonderful bond of connection because "there is kind of a sisterhood and brotherhood amongst us." For her, this has filled some of the void that was created by not knowing her heritage.

We are drawn to one another

Not only are we like family…we are drawn together, like bees to honey. A friend of mine said that his preschooler seemed to sense when other kids were adopted, and whenever he peeked in on her at preschool, she was playing with them.

Kathy says she became good friends with another adoptee, unknowingly. When they got to be good enough friends that they shared secrets with one another, lo and behold, guess what the secret was! They were both adopted. What a wonderful relationship that turned out to be. Kathy says God continues to bring fellow adoptees into her life as the years go by.

"When I was in college, I had three adopted roommates," says Connie Dawson:

> I had known my freshman roommate in high school and knew she was adopted, although we never actually talked about adoption. I guess I unknowingly attracted two other roommates who were adopted and I didn't know it until later, perhaps because there was some very subterranean connection or way of being. Who knows? But when I came to learn more about adoption and what it meant to my development, I thought my roommate selection was interesting!

Kimberly Steiner says that her best friend is a fellow Korean adoptee and that she is part of three Korean adoptee support groups. It all started when she went to a gathering for first-generation adoptees from Korea. What a joy for her to find so many people with commonality as well as diversity. She was stretched emotionally, and everything she believed about adoption was challenged and is now positive.

We have a unique emotional language

Renee Mills says she values friendships with other adoptees because she is able to speak about adoption experiences and know that the other person "gets it."

College student Melinda Faust says, "My cousin Kelly is the same age as I am and is also adopted. Always having someone there who completely understands has been really important."

Cheri Freeman says that fellow adoptees can "read" each other from just a few words or their body language, which makes them feel like they belong to each other. "And that's a good thing when you don't feel you belong anywhere else," she concludes.

Bob Blanchard stresses the importance of these relationships because he has found much insight about personality traits that are common among adoptees. He has found it so beneficial to be able to discuss these things with others who have "been there."

Jody Moreen says that even though adoptees' circumstances are unique, they share some of the same feelings and emotions. She has become more keenly aware of this since attending and leading adoption support groups with other adoptees. When one is sharing his or her adoption story, you can look up and see the heads of other adoptees nodding in understanding and agreement. "There seems to be an 'emotional language' only understood by another adoptee who has walked a mile in our shoes."

Deb Bryan was amazed at the immediate connection she felt to fellow adoptees upon first meeting them—more of a connection than to folks she had known for years.

We can vent feelings

Not only do we feel comfortable in communicating with one another, but we can also blow off steam in safety. Kim Norman can be brutally honest with her fellow adoptees, and being with them surfaces issues that might otherwise be neglected, ignored, or denied. Going to support group meetings keeps her in touch with the tough issues she wants to resolve.

Paula Oliver says that it's so much easier to explain what she is feeling to someone who has been through it personally. She finds relief when talking with fellow adoptees who can wrap words around her emotions and give her the freedom to express all her feelings and frustrations.

We don't need to explain ourselves

Another wonderful benefit of our relationships is that we don't need to explain ourselves to one another—there's just kind of a "knowing."

"As an adoptee, my friendships with other adoptees have been wonderful because we understand each other and can easily have empathy for each other," says Joe Soll.

Connie Dawson agrees that it's a relief not to have to explain herself or protect herself from the judgments she feels are so often there when someone "finds out" she's adopted. "It's very subtle," Connie says. "It may have something to do with adoptees being 'rejects' or something. Sometimes I think people feel, at some primitive level, that we have experienced abandonment and they pull back because their worst fear is being abandoned. And we've already experienced it."

Phyllis-Anne Munro says that her adoptee friend gave her a sense of security and safety in his presence, even though they didn't talk about adoption.

Alex brings up a crucial point. He says that it is truly a joy to be with fellow adoptees but under one condition: that they are growing, open, aware, and eager to know about the complexities of adoption. These dynamics, he says, produce the "knowing" about one another that needs no explanation.

If you don't have a fellow-adoptee friend, you don't know what you're missing.

Why we need one another

Now let's shift gears a bit and focus on the title of this chapter— "An Hour with a Fellow Adoptee Is Better Than Weeks of Therapy." In preceding chapters, we've discussed loss issues at length, and I think it is safe to conclude that the majority of us struggle to one degree or another with fears of rejection and abandonment.

Why do I bring this up *again*? Because many of us find help for these fears in psychotherapy, at least in the US. It's part of our culture. In other cultures it may not be, or you may not be able to afford it.

Psychotherapy certainly has its place in helping many of us become whole, and often creates an environment where we have the guts to let down the I-have-it-all-together façade and be real.

However, there are distinct limitations involved in psychotherapy that are not inherent in adoptee-to-adoptee relationships and support. This is encouraging for those in countries where therapy isn't on every street corner, or those who can't afford it—there's something better.

Therapy is temporary

The first is the fact that therapy is temporary. You know what I discovered after seven *long* years of therapy and thousands of dollars under the bridge? At the end of one-hour appointments, all I could see was the therapist's backside leaving the room for the next appointment! I was just one of many clients and this was a business relationship to them, whereas for me it was personal and I had become extremely attached.

Yes, I learned what it meant to feel safe. Yes, I learned how to open up. Yes, I learned to trust. Yes, my life was changed tremendously by professional coaching and mentoring. But eventually, whether it is after seven months or seven years of treatment, the relationship ends. For many adoptees, the "goodbye" at the end of therapy can be a huge trigger for abandonment issues.

Therapy can be limited

It is vitally important for the therapist to help us grieve the loss of that trusted relationship. But even that process can fall short. Why?

First, because "termination," no matter how well done, often translates as loss and rejection for many of us. For that reason, we are much more likely to handle stopping therapy with peace of mind if it doesn't feel so final. Fellow adoptee Dr. Joyce Maguire Pavao suggests what I suspect is the best way for adoptees and therapists to part. "There is a completion of each stage of therapy, but no 'termination,'" Pavao advises. "The word 'terminate' is too loaded for those who have suffered the losses associated with adoption. The therapist or team of therapists remains available for consultation and therapy. This avoids the emotional cut-off and loss that are primary issues in adoption."[1]

The second reason therapy can fall short is because most physicians and therapists haven't been specifically trained to know how loss impacts adoptees. Dr. Pavao said in an article in *Family Therapy News*:

> There is no real training in professional schools regarding adoption. In social work programs, there is perhaps one case study. Certainly, there is nothing in marriage and family therapy or psychology graduate programs, unless someone makes it his or her dissertation. Even then, it is hard to find faculty who understand the issues and have experience in this field. In the American medical school curriculum, there are only two or three paragraphs about adoption. The American Association for Marriage and Family Therapy (AAMFT) occasionally offers one or two workshops on adoption at its national conference.

But this subject is under-represented at all mental health conferences.[2]

I must add here that there *is* a national association of adoption pediatricians. I didn't know that until I attended a recent conference. So the medical field is coming along! Still, I don't believe there is any doctor or therapist who can understand an adoptee like a fellow adoptee *unless* that professional just happens to be an adoptee. And not just *any* adoptee, but one who is dealing with adoption-related issues on a personal, ongoing, proactive basis.

One of my friends entered a therapy relationship believing that because the therapist was also adopted, she would "get it." But she didn't. This therapist had not done her own emotional work. The result was that my friend terminated therapy and found what she needed through adoptee support groups and friendships.

The crème-de-la-crème therapist is a fellow adoptee who *has been* and *is currently* learning and growing from his or her adoption experience. Not only can that person relate to our issues on a personal level, but they can also weave in appropriate, psychological principles that provide insight that's tailor-made for an adoptee. However, these individuals are rare and difficult to find. Connie Dawson, Dirck Brown, Joe Soll, Joyce Maguire Pavao, and Betty Jean Lifton fall into this category and have been such a blessing in the therapeutic world.

Adoptee friendships last

Even if we're fortunate to have the most effective therapy and closure possible, we still need a huge safety net to fall into, like the kind they have at the circus for tightrope walkers. That safety net is relationships with fellow adoptees. Certainly the tools I was taught in therapy to use are ones I will always use. But as far as relationships go, adoptee friends are my *permanent* source of support.

Adoptee friendships are great because we never have to say goodbye. We can seek out one another and stay connected indefinitely because our relationships are not business-related, but personal.

Richard Curtis has found this to be true and has put it into action. Some years ago seventeen male adoptees from around the country met at the annual session of the AAC. At the end of the session they realized what a rare experience their annual all-male meeting created for ninety minutes. But it was so temporary because once the convention was over the group disbursed and didn't have contact until the next convention.

"But that year was different!" says Richard. "We created an ongoing email system (AACMA—American Adoption Congress Male Adoptees) linking us to each other, whereby we can correspond any time with the entire group or with individual members."

After reflecting on the potential depth of our relationships with each other and the limitations of therapy, wouldn't you agree with me that an hour with a fellow adoptee who is growing like we are can far surpass weeks of psychotherapy? Besides, it's free…and fun.

Our Choice

To connect in meaningful, supportive relationships with at least one fellow adoptee.

"Well, how am I going to do that?" you may be asking. "I live way out in the boonies where there probably isn't an adoptee for miles." Here are some ways to begin.

How to begin

- *Find an adoptee Intensive Care Unit (ICU).* There are many all-adoptee groups online. Just Google search to find.

   I would like to tell you about my favorite site! It is the jewel among jewels adoption network site (all-adoptees@ yahoogroups.com).

   It is my personal favorite because it is Biblically based (but not "in your face"). The *Under His Wings* workbook is used there, so it's not just a dumping place for feelings and beliefs, and there's a healthy structure. However, there are plenty of other groups and you should be able to find the right one for you.

   I believe that we adoptees need an ICU before we are in a group with others whose lives have been touched by adoption. We need a safe place to vent where we don't have to worry about hurting others, and a good, structured support group can serve as such a place.

- *Attend a local, national, or international adoption conference.* This will be a life-changing experience for you!

Yes, there's something unspoken that draws us together, like magnets to metal. We share a common interest and we can huddle together in amazement as we see our common, ordinary lives gradually transform into something extraordinary, like the bud of a flower opening into a full bloom. Whenever we see each other and enter into that secret place of mutual understanding, every moment is cherished, and we are invigorated in ways we never dreamed possible.

As we hear the stories of other adoptees and how adoption as well as reunion has impacted their lives, we may begin thinking about the possibility of a reunion with our own birth families. However, there is an obstacle we must overcome before considering that possibility. We'll cover that next.

True guilt is guilt at the obligation one owes to oneself to be oneself. False guilt is guilt felt at not being what other people feel one ought to be or assume that one is.

—R.D. LAING

CHAPTER twelve

False Guilt Shouldn't Stop Us from Considering a Reunion

Connection! Connection with our past, with our heritage. This is our *most* basic need as adoptees. But because we can become so enmeshed in false guilt, our innate need for thinking about a reunion with our birth families is shoved beneath our consciousness.

Drs. David Brodzinsky and Marshall Schechter say, "Connectedness to an adopted person is like water to a person in the desert. You spend your whole life having it hidden, denied, and desecrated."[1]

Do you think this is true? Is it true that we *keep it hidden*? Oh, yes. Many of us don't think we should have such a desire, so we hold it close to our chests, like a good hand in a card game. It's another one of our adoptee secrets.

Is it true that we *deny* our need? I believe this is true also.

How? By putting up smoke screens. "Oh, the only reason I want to search is for medical reasons. I don't want a relationship with my birth mother."

You know what I say to adoptees who say this to me? "Hogwash! You really want to find your birth mother but are afraid to admit it."

There is a deep yearning within us to connect. Getting medical information is important but secondary.

Brodzinsky and Schechter say that they are often asked what percentage of adoptees search for their birth parents. Their answer:

> One hundred percent. In our experience, *all* adoptees engage in a search process. It may not be a literal search, but it is a meaningful search nonetheless. It begins when the child first asks, 'Why did it happen?' 'Who are they?' 'Where are they now?' These questions may be asked out loud, or they may constitute a more private form of searching—questions that are examined only in the solitude of self-reflection. The universal search begins during early school years, prompted by the child's growing awareness of adoption issues.[2]

And how about the *desecration* part?

First of all, what does that word mean? My dictionary says, "To divert from a sacred to a profane use or purpose."[3] What is it that is sacred? I believe it is our very lives and life purposes. Would it be correct to assume that connection with our birth families is sacred? I have never thought about it that way, but I think it is a beautiful concept.

Just think back to Chapter Three, where we shared our innermost thoughts about our birth parents. Love in the purest human form came through the words on those pages. No matter what the circumstances of our conception or our experiences with our birth parents after birth and on into life, a deep love for them still exists, which results in a need for connection in *some* form. Because we have dual identities, it's impossible to think about our life purpose without including our birth families.

Why, then, is our desire for connection hidden, denied, and desecrated? I believe it's because of a phenomenon called "false guilt." This is not psychobabble, but instead a psychological reality hidden in the deepest regions of our adoptee hearts. It's irrational and illusive and the constant companion of many throughout life, even though we may not know its name.

False guilt is something we feel responsible for, over which we have or had no control. Dr. Paul Brand, a missionary physician and author, likens false guilt to phantom pain. He says:

> Amputees often experience some sensation of a phantom limb. Somewhere, locked in their brains, a memory lingers of the non-existent hand or leg. Invisible toes curl, imaginary hands grasp things, and a 'leg' feels so sturdy a patient may try to stand on it. Doctors watch helplessly, for the part of the body screaming for attention…does not exist.[4]

The messages of false guilt

What is it that we are truly responsible for? For many of us, that question leads to the messages of false guilt. How can we recognize these condemning messages and then, once we do, how can we get rid of them?

"YOU are responsible!"

Responsible for what? The message is so vague, yet haunting. Dr. Richard B. Gilbert says, "There is the innocence of a child, even an adult child, to hold on to what isn't in order to fix it."

False guilt takes a sacred purpose—our lives—and tells us that we are responsible for the circumstances surrounding our conceptions and births. "YOU were conceived in rape!" "YOU were an unplanned pregnancy" "YOU are illegitimate."

The result? We subconsciously believe we have no right to be alive.

"You have no right to be alive"

The truth, of course, is that we had *absolutely no control* over the circumstances of our conceptions and births. Our parents did.

Kimberly Steiner silently blamed herself for her conception and being abandoned, concluding that there was something wrong with her that made her mother give her up. Either she did something wrong, wasn't large enough, wasn't pretty enough, or wasn't quite enough. Somehow she didn't measure up to her birth mother's standards.

What has given me comfort about this is a verse in the New Testament that says God created *all* things. In fact, it says, "Without him nothing was made that has been made."[5] This reassures me that I am not a mistake; I am supposed to be here; I am included in the *all*. That's true for each and every one of us.

"Justify your existence by helping others"

If we take another step into false guilt, we believe that we must prove our worth. This often takes the form of unhealthy caretaking—tending to others' needs and desires at the expense of our own well-being.

Connie Dawson says that if she were to speak realistically about her parents, she would say that they were emotionally immature and needy. They complained about their lives, but did nothing to deal with what they were complaining about. She thinks this is important because her mother had suffered three unsuccessful pregnancies before Connie was adopted, and she doesn't believe her parents ever grieved their losses. They had so much repressed grief that Connie picked up their pain and tried to take care of it, never wanting to be the cause of them "feeling bad."

Her mother also shoved responsibility on to Connie for her dad's anger and anxiety. "No wonder I learned to stake my existence on how well I could relieve the stress of others," says Connie, "to the exclusion of myself, of course. The trouble with adapting by being so 'helpful' is that I didn't develop my identity aside from being the helpmate."

Richard Curtis says he was the caretaker in all of his relationships. And why not? He had learned those traits well in his adoptive home, desperately seeking to be loved by an adoptive mother who herself needed help in dealing with the loss of her husband and two stillborn children. As a child, Richard could not provide this kind of help, of course. He lived in terror and felt that survival in his home depended on taking care of his emotionally broken mom.

"Our pain and shame are your fault"

Another lie of false guilt is that we are responsible for our birth parents' pain and shame.

After the unsuccessful reunion with my birth mother, whenever I told my story I felt heaviness come over me, like I was at the funeral of someone I love. One day I realized how erroneous some of my beliefs were. I said to myself, *Sherrie, you're accepting your birth mother's pain and rejection and carrying her shame. You don't have to do that any longer. You can choose to forgive and cut her loose.*

So now when I tell my story, I say, "I have no relationship with my birth mother." And I leave it at that.

"You are guilty, guilty, guilty"

If we are people of faith, we may confess everything possible before God, yet retain an indefinable sense of guilt. We may even believe that God has forgiven us, yet this nagging guilt plagues us. I know one adoptee who begins practically every sentence with "I am sorry but…"

Sandy Garrett says that she treated her adoptive mom horribly as a teen and later her mom died, leaving Sandy with a lot of guilt, wondering if her mom ever knew Sandy loved her. What made it doubly confusing for Sandy is that now she is reunited with her birth mother, she treats her like she *should* have treated her adoptive mom. Sandy says, "I constantly worry that my adoptive mom is watching over me and is hurt by how nice I am to my birth mom."

I have learned to bypass false guilt by choosing to believe what the apostle John says in the New Testament:

> If we claim that we're free of sin, we're only fooling ourselves. A claim like that is errant nonsense. On the other hand, if we admit our sins—make a clean breast of them—he won't let us down; he'll be true to himself. He'll forgive our sins and purge us of all wrongdoing.[6]

If I confess my wrongs to God and guilt keeps haunting me, it's a dead giveaway that I'm carrying false guilt.

Ways we can be liberated from false guilt

Maybe now is the time to change. I have seen it happen time after time in adoptee support groups. People listen to the stories of fellow adoptees, and when they hear various reunion stories, they start to feel free to think about their own.

Hearing another adoptee's story

That's what happened to me. When I read about how God himself brought Moses' birth brother, Aaron, back into his life in response to Moses' whining about being incompetent for the task God had set before him, I was encouraged. God told the stuttering Moses, "I know he can speak well. He is already on his way to meet you, and his heart will be glad when he sees you."[7]

Moses had a choice at that point. He could either open himself up to a reunion with his birth brother—and to fulfilling God's will with his brother beside him—or he could continue to hide out in the desert. Moses made the right choice, and God honored it in countless ways.

"Being a person of faith, I needed to surrender this desire to God," Jody Moreen says. "I desired a confirmation that it was indeed his will that I search for my birth family and history. In time I felt assurance when I read in the Bible, 'Then you will know the truth, and the truth will set you free.'"[8]

Believing we deserve good things

Another act that sets us free from false guilt is allowing our deepest dreams and desires to surface, and to start believing we deserve to have our unmet needs met.

Let me ask you this: have you ever become aware of a deep desire, yet feared having that desire fulfilled?

I remember when Bob and I were planning our shotgun wedding. My dad asked if I wanted a big wedding. No. I was too ashamed. I wanted to get it over with as soon as possible. Just recently, a friend reframed this for me and said I was showing integrity.

But as the years went by, I became very sorry that I didn't have a formal wedding, with a big white dress to wear down the aisle on Dad's arm. I always dreamed of that dress, but whenever I did, I got an ache in the pit of my stomach. It was something I could have had, but didn't because I didn't think I deserved it.

When Bob and I were planning our twenty-fifth anniversary celebration, we decided to have a ceremony at church, invite family and a few friends, and renew our vows. Months before the anniversary, when I was in Bob's hometown of Fowler, Michigan, I drove by the bridal shop and saw a beautiful white lace, over-the-knee-length dress with a white satin ribbon around the waist. I sneaked into the shop like a little kid and tried it on. It was a perfect fit.

Did I buy it?

No.

Why?

I still didn't think I deserved it.

When talking with my counselor about it and telling her what the options were for twenty-fifth anniversary attire, she simply said, "I think you should get the white dress."

No sooner had she said the words than I was sobbing like a baby. I ended up buying and wearing the dress, and I still have it hanging in my closet (even though I can't get it zipped anymore!).

So many of us are a lot like I was when it comes to considering an adoption reunion for ourselves. Deep within our hearts is the need and desire to connect, but because of the way in which we came into this world, we don't believe we deserve it. What a lie!

Would you let me say to you, dear friends, in essence what my therapist said to me? "I think you deserve something wonderful."

We need to listen to our hearts…they're crying out for that basic connection every human being needs and deserves. In response, what life-giving choice can we make?

Our Choice

To weed out false guilt and begin thinking about how to meet our basic need for connection with our heritage.

How to begin

- *Make a searching inventory of your responsibilities.* On a sheet of paper list everything and everybody you are responsible for. (On second thoughts, maybe you should get two pieces of paper!) Divide the paper into four columns and label them: *Responsibility: What is my motivation behind taking on this responsibility? How do I feel when I am carrying out this responsibility? Am I really responsible for this?* Then, review your whole inventory and look for patterns. Many adoptees take on "stuff" that isn't theirs. Could this exercise help you let go of things you're doing that aren't truly your responsibility?

- *Read reunion stories.* Go to your local library or download an e-book and read about the experiences of others in regard to reunion. I will never forget reading my first adoption book. I can't remember the title but it was about a young woman who was in a medical crisis and needing desperately to connect with birth relatives. After reading the stories of others, dare to dream of your own!

Clearing our minds of false guilt may lead us to the next step in our process where we may feel torn between our birth and adoptive parents. We'll tackle that hurdle next.

Trials teach us what we are; they dig up the soil, and let us see what we are made of.

—CHARLES SPURGEON

CHAPTER thirteen

Search and Reunion May Become a Top Priority

The plane touched down in Reno at 8:00 p.m. Exhausted, I planned on going straight to the hotel after renting a car, but something else took precedence over my rest…reuniting with my dying birth brother, Jon C. Perry.

Even though I knew Jon's contact information years prior to this evening, I didn't have peace about searching for him. It was different now. I couldn't get there fast enough.

My brother was a Facebook find! We talked every night prior to my trip and he assured me that even though we were half siblings, "I don't do halves. You're my sis, and that's it."

After punching his address into the car's GPS, I traveled into the worst section of town to find the trailer home he shared with his wife, Dorothy. What would I find behind the closed door? She opened it, gave me a hug, and invited me in. Behind her was a scene I will never forget. She was a hoarder.

"Sis," Jon said, voice wavering while embracing me. "You are so beautiful."

Lovable beyond belief, he looked like a hippie who had never changed with the times—long gray hair and a beard to his chest.

We talked until midnight, sharing details of life. Of course, we had the common bond of a cruel mother. I met her at midlife but Jon was raised by her and suffered much abuse. I was older than Jon, the oldest of all the children my birth mother delivered. Adoption took me away from her, which I was becoming more grateful for by the hour.

The next morning, upon arrival at the trailer, Dorothy came running out, hysterical. "They've taken Jon to the hospital."

Reno's Renown Hospital had already admitted Jon, where they could pump his veins with painkillers for his incredibly swollen belly.

I am sure it was terribly embarrassing to him for me to see him this way. Earlier in life, he was a man's man, an artist, a dad, and professional painter, managing more than 50 men. Back in the day, he was incredibly handsome. He still was to me.

I loved him so.

After a few hours, he was released and I took him and Dorothy home. The days that followed were nothing short of miraculous. It was his birthday week and mine, so we planned a family dinner at a restaurant. We piled into my car and Dorothy shopped at Walmart for a new outfit and then both her and Jon got wonderful haircuts at a walk-in salon.

I thought I might explode with joy.

The honeymoon stage of reunion

Everywhere Jon and I went, we'd say, "We just found one another!" Without exception, everyone wanted to hear our reunion story. The frosting on the cake was when we were interviewed by a Reno television station about our reunion. Jon told them I was more than a sister. I was also like a mom. That figures…I didn't know how to be a sister! Remember, I was an only child, always wanting a sibling?

Our birthday party a few days later was wonderful, and we vowed to celebrate every future birthday together. After dinner, we had family portraits taken at a local department store.

Then it was time to say goodbye. After many hugs, we parted, for the flight back home was early the next morning. Jon broke into tears and I numbed out, thinking only about the next time we'd be together.

We talked via phone every day after that, and he always ended every phone call with "Sis, I love you with all my heart."

Summer was nearing and the time we would see one another again. We were going to go to his favorite place to get me some cowboy boots. Of course, he was the expert! Also, I was going to play some kind of trick on him because during our first days together, he and his son, Jon, took me to an Asian restaurant and encouraged me to get a certain kind of soup. Later, they cracked up telling me it had cow eyeballs in it.

However, one morning I got a call from Reno Renown Hospital.

"Aunt Sherrie," my new-found nephew said. "Dad is on life support."

"I'll be on the next flight," I responded breathlessly.

"No, you can't. It's too late," Jon said. "Aunt Sherrie…he's already gone, Aunt Sherrie. There is no brain activity."

My knees buckled.

Then, Jon's wife asked if I wanted to say goodbye to him via phone, reminding me that hearing is the last thing to go before death. She put the phone up to his ear.

"Jon, I love you with all my heart. I know you know that. I am so glad that we got to meet. You filled a hole in my heart that I never knew was there. I always wanted a brother and never dreamed I'd have one, especially one like you. I love you…I love you…I love you. I will see you in heaven."

When I found my brother through Facebook, it was a relatively new phenomenon. Now, it's common. And, with the prevalence of searching via social media, it can be very risky and dangerous.

Here are some thoughts to consider if you're searching through social media.

Five social media landmines

I believe all of us adoptees are searching for lost relatives, even if subconsciously. With the growth of social media, it is commonplace to find a lost relative. Connections might occur, creating an emotional high, but often there are landmines for which no one is prepared.

Here are five landmines for adoptees searching for lost birth relatives through social media:

- **Landmine #1: Euphoric reactions.** Adoption experts say that the need adoptees have for connection can be compared to a starving man looking for food. Many adoptees have been looking for a birth relative for a lifetime, and once that connection is made, euphoria sets in. This is the time to harness those emotions. This surely is a blood relative, but you have no history or relationship yet.

- **Landmine #2: Impulsive decisions.** Yes, it has taken a lifetime and you may want to hop on the next plane headed for your birth relative's home. But don't rush into it! It is wise to take things slowly, get to know the person through photos, phone calls, and Skype.

- **Landmine #3: Unrealistic expectations.** Most adoptees are famous for creating fantasies about lost birth relatives. The adoptee may believe the birth mother is a queen living in a castle, and the birth father a knight coming to the rescue on a white horse.

- **Landmine #4: Over-confidence.** Adoptees may consider themselves healthy emotionally and relationally. Yet meeting a birth relative for the first time usually sends an adoptee back to core issues such as fear of rejection and anger.

- **Landmine #5: Intensity and lack of self-care.** Because adoptees have looked for a lifetime, they are on a mission to get the hole in their hearts filled with this missing person. They would likely do anything for this person. The result is lack of self-care and disappointment.

Questions to ask yourself

One of the most difficult things to do is to slow down when we're in an emotional state. So, here are some questions to tuck away for those times:

- Do I really want to share my personal details with the entire world?

- Am I aware that people can present themselves any way they desire on social media and that it is possible to be fooled?

- Am I approaching this search like I would a literal search? Is there an intermediary involved so birth mothers aren't shocked? Have letters of intent been sent, assuring family that you want nothing…just to meet them? Wait for replies even though you are anxious to hear back.

Reunion in retrospect

Reflecting on personal experience, I've known both rejection and unconditional love from birth family members. These are a few realities that have clarified things for me. Maybe they will be of some help to you. I hope so.

- Adoptees are often rejected by birth mothers, especially if their history involves the closed adoption system. It is common but not discussed in the media.

- If birth mothers haven't grieved loss, they can't welcome adoptees with open arms and hearts.

- Reunion is always a risk and step of faith.

- No matter what the opposition from family or friends, an adoptee must follow his or her heart if it leads to reunion. None of us wants to be on our death bed wishing we had searched.

- Sibling reunions usually don't carry as much heavy emotional baggage as parental reunions.

- Reunion is not the panacea for adoptees. It doesn't erase the fact that we are adopted.

- Open adoption is not the panacea either. Adoptees still experience loss and rejection, perhaps on a more consistent basis.

- Realistically, having both families in your life changes your lifestyle: more relatives, and relatives at family gatherings who may not want to be mixed together.

How to prepare for reunion

- Identify expectations before and during the time with your new-found family member.

- Don't act on emotion…go slowly. That is one thing I wish I could have changed in the reunion with my birth mother.

- Always have someone with you.

- Meet in a neutral place…that way no one has control.

- Make the first meeting short and sweet. Ice cream for an hour.

- Make sure to have a support network in place with people you can text or call at any given moment. There will be times when you feel vulnerable and need someone else's perspective.

Certainly, you could all add many other points, but perhaps these can be springboards for thought and discussion. Ultimately, we are at a choice point.

Our Choice

To pace ourselves as we experience search and reunion.

How to begin

- *Care for yourself during this time.* It is very stressful, so get good sleep and exercise. Stay balanced. Only allow an allotted time for searching.

- *Give up the expectation that you'll find answers to every adoption question.* That won't happen for any of us this side of heaven.

- *Start by sharing only a few things about yourself.* When you first reunite with birth relatives, share only a few things about yourself, but ask many questions. It's so easy to turn them off by blurting out your entire story.

- *Realize that every birth family member reunion is different and unique.* I thought I was a pro at it by the time I met my birth brother, but I wasn't. It is always "unexplored territory." Walk humbly.

There's one thing that should always be in place before searching and reuniting—we will feel a tug in our hearts and minds concerning our birth and adoptive parents. Let's talk about that next.

Adoptees are caught between the loyalty they feel to the adoptive parents who rescued them and the invisible loyalty to the mother who gave them birth.

—BETTY JEAN LIFTON

CHAPTER fourteen

We Don't Need to Fear Seeming Ungrateful or Disloyal

Have you ever stretched a rubber band between your hands as far as possible? You pull in opposite directions, taking a deep breath because you're afraid the band is going to break. When you're near the breaking point, you let go because you don't want to get snapped.

Well, what happens if *you* are that rubber band and are being pulled in opposite directions out of loyalty to both sets of parents—adoptive and birth? This is another issue that involves our dual identity, and coming to terms with it means that we must learn that it's all right to talk about our birth parents to our adoptive parents.

Struggles with loyalty are common among adoptees; in fact, some of us may be experiencing those feelings right now. So let's take a look at what loyalty issues really are and how they affect our relationships with our adoptive parents.

A loyalty issue occurs when we feel we must be protective of our adoptive parents. We perceive that any verbalization of our feelings about our birth parents would be a knife through their hearts. Yet we naturally long to know our birth families. We wonder, "Is it permissible or possible to be loyal to both?"

Synonyms for "loyal" are: "faithful, allegiant, true-hearted, devoted, pledged, dedicated, steadfast, unchanging, firm, stable, solid, supportive."[1] Knowing this, where does our struggle originate? Is it just "built in" to us as adoptees because of the dynamics of adoption, or could negative reactions of adoptive parents be a contributing factor?

Lori Ann Pewsey knows full well that asking even a few questions about her birth family will cause problems, so she hasn't told her mother she is searching. As a child, when Lori *did* ask her mother those few questions, she got the quivering-lip, teary-eyed response. Her mother would say in a hurt tone, "Why would you ever want to know?" Since that time, Lori knew that her desire and quest to find her birth family would have to be her secret.

Kenny Tucker says, "My adoptive parents have chosen not to meet my biological parents, so there's some sense of ignoring the 'elephant' in the living room when I'm with my adoptive parents or my biological family comes up in conversation."

What we may believe about loyalty

Kim Norman felt the tug of loyalty at an early age. She says, "I do remember feeling guilt about expressing thoughts about my birth parents to my adoptive parents when I was young. I felt insecure about how they would react to my initiating a discussion out of my curiosity."

Melissa started thinking about her birth mother when she learned about her adoption at the age of sixteen. Although she felt she had the right to think about her birth family, she also felt guilt, fearing she was being disloyal to her adoptive parents. She was fortunate to have a loving family with the added bonus of being raised with a biological sibling, but she still felt guilt.

Loyalty issues can also begin as we contemplate searching. If they have begun by then, they often intensify as we move closer to reunion.

Even though Renee Mills's adoptive father has been dead for thirteen years, she hasn't told her adoptive mother that she is going to meet her birth father in just a few months. She describes her mother as "fiercely protective of my dad's memory," and Renee is sure her mother would say she was betraying her dead father by seeking out her birth father.

Many feel we must choose between the two families

As adoptees, we may be confused about to whom we are supposed to be loyal. Many of us have a special place in our hearts for our birth parents, yet we fear that talking about them—or even thinking about them—is an act of disloyalty to our adoptive parents. We feel caught between a rock and a hard place because we believe we must choose between the two.

Rebecca L. Ricardo says:

I can remember thinking as a young child of six or seven that my birth parents could come and find me and that I would have to choose between them and my adoptive parents. This was a choice I did not feel I could ever make.

Lisa Storms says she doesn't feel safe talking about her roller coaster emotions to her adoptive parents since she has started searching. She says they are more interested in the facts of the search than in how she is feeling. This has caused her to hold back emotionally, the result being that she feels she has to choose between her two sets of parents.

We fear we might create misunderstandings

It took Jody Moreen a year after starting her search to share the news with her adoptive parents. Because her relationship with them was warm and loving, she feared creating a misunderstanding. However, after the initial shock, they encouraged her to carry on.

Paula Oliver says that she didn't want to hurt her folks, but when she finally decided to go ahead with her search, much to her delight her parents were very supportive and even expressed that they wished they had more information to give her.

Emmary Nicholson says:

> I haven't told my adoptive dad that I was reunited, even a year after my birth mom passed away. I *do* want to tell him though. Loyalty to my adoptive dad is also why I haven't pursued a relationship with my biological dad. I've written him a letter that went unanswered. I haven't done anything since then to contact him.

We fear appearing ungrateful

We are in the midst of loyalty issues when we are struggling with thoughts like, "They have given me everything when I had nothing." "I was an orphan and they gave me a roof over my head and plenty of love." "I long to talk about my birth parents but I feel I owe all my allegiance to my adoptive parents."

Sue says that when she found her birth parents, she didn't tell her adoptive parents, concluding that they would see it as an act of betrayal on her part, an example of her not having any gratitude for the great life they had worked hard to provide. Guilt plagued her. "Yet I *needed* to search," Sue says.

We feel sneaky and guilty

Another loyalty issue is the feeling that we are being sneaky. We feel like traitors.

I can't begin to tell you how sneaky I felt that day I drove out of my dad's driveway, turned the car as if heading for Indiana, but went instead to the county courthouse. There I was, a grown woman, still feeling like she had to sneak around like a child. I felt like my parents were in the living room and I was in the kitchen trying to quietly get my hand in the cookie jar for a treat. How dare I sneak around looking for a cookie when I had a dad who loved me so much he would have done anything for me? What would Dad do if he found out? I was afraid he might become angry. After all, I was their one and only child and I didn't think he would want to share me with anyone.

Cheri Freeman felt sneaky when she found her birth mother's last name on the "receipt" for her adoption. She didn't mention it to her adoptive parents, but years later, when she was ready to search, she asked a friend to pose as her birth mother at the hospital where she was born to illegally verify the last name and obtain the first name of her birth mother. As she began her actual search, Cheri wondered if her late mother would approve of her decision. In preparing for a move, Cheri's daughter found Cheri's birth mother's name written on the inside of her baby book, which was proof that her mom knew the name all along. This brought Cheri great peace, believing that this was her mom's way of giving permission for her to search for her birth family.

Connie Dawson says:

Would it be enough to say I waited until my dad had died and my mother was in a nursing home? When I contacted my birth family, I did so without telling my mother. I felt so sneaky but my counselor helped me realize that my belief that I had to protect [my adoptive parents] at the cost of my own needs was like a 'condition of life' for me. As an adult, I could, of course, make different decisions from those I made as a child, but I've been surprised by how strongly I felt I was being disloyal and untrue to them and to myself.

How to resolve loyalty issues

After listening to these struggles, wouldn't you say that it's time that we gained some kind of peace and autonomy? As adoptees, we have the *right* and oftentimes the *need* to be loyal to *both* sets of parents. Having a dual identity is a fundamental fact of our uniqueness.

If we're allowing ourselves to be pulled in both directions, what is the answer? Do we live in a state of stress and tension all our lives, feeling like we have to walk on eggshells when it comes to the topic of our birth parents? No, we don't!

Let's go back first to the opening illustration of the rubber band. We have determined that we know what it feels like to be that rubber band. But what would happen if we could cut that band? What if we made the decision to verbalize our thoughts and feelings to our adoptive parents without reservation? Talking about our birth families is *not* tantamount to mutiny! Instead, it's a sign that we are beginning to integrate the dual aspects of our identity…and that's good!

Resolving loyalty issues is a difficult task because we have an ingrained belief that we need to take care of our adoptive parents' feelings. We need to consciously remind ourselves that they are big people and can take care of themselves. In addition, we need to give up trying to control them for fear they will reject us. We can't control *anyone's* responses, except our own. Accepting that fact is taking a big step toward maturity.

When loyalty issues come up, we can use self-talk to remind ourselves. This is a loyalty issue and it feels very uncomfortable.

But giving up control of how my parents react is what I must do in order to grow. Do I want to grow? Yes…but I will experience growing pains along the way, especially regarding this issue.

I am reminded of a passage in the New Testament that talks about what true love is. Part of it goes like this: Love "takes pleasure in the flowering of truth, puts up with anything, trusts God always, always looks for the best, never looks back, but keeps going to the end."[2]

Is loving like this going to be easy? Read on with me:

> When I was an infant at my mother's breast, I gurgled and cooed like any infant. When I grew up, I left those infant ways for good. We don't yet see things clearly. We're squinting in a fog, peering through a mist. But it won't be long before the weather clears and the sun shines bright![3]

It isn't going to be easy, but Maggie Bachiewicz, age seven, gives us hope that adoptees *can* work through this conundrum of divided loyalties. She says, "I don't feel guilty for thinking and talking about my birth family. It doesn't mean I love my adoptive family any less!"

Ah…from the mouths of babes!

And so what is our choice about this loyalty business?

Our Choice

To freely discuss our birth families with our adoptive parents, and vice versa.

The rubber band has been cut by our own choosing! The pressure is off. We are moving toward more and more freedom! Every time we recognize a loyalty issue, we can give thanks that we are unique creations with a dual heritage, and that even though it is often difficult for others to understand or accept, we can feel confident that this is our life path.

How to begin

Make a list of statements and behaviors that create "rubber band" feelings and reactions. Following each statement, write a healthy response. Here are several to get you started:

- **"Why would you want to meet THEM?"**

  "Because they are a part of me and not knowing them makes me feel empty inside."

  "The puzzle of my life is missing pieces and I need to find them to complete it."

  "They gave me my body and my first home. Why wouldn't I want to meet them?"

- **"Leave us out of this…you can search, but we don't want any part of it."**

  "That's fine, Mom and Dad. I respect your choice."

  "You are free to do whatever you want."

  "The decision is up to you."

- **"Why would you want to do THAT?"**

  "I want to talk about and meet my birth parents because they are an integral part of my life."

  "Because they gave me the gift of life."

"Because I have a special place in my heart for them."

- **"I guess it means that we didn't do a good enough job as your parents."**

  "It's not about your parenting; it's about my needs."

  "Parenting skills have nothing to do with my choice."

  "I wish you didn't feel that way."

- **"Why would you want to open THAT can of worms?"**

  "It hurts me when you refer to my birth family as a can of worms."

  "When you refer to them as a can of worms, I feel unloved. Please don't say it again."

- **"Do whatever—it's no big deal to us. We really don't care."**

  "It may not be a big deal to you, but it is to me."

  "That's a pretty unloving thing to say."

  "I wish you did care, but I can't control your thoughts."

- **Complete silence when we talk about birth families.**

  "If you don't want to talk about it, that's okay with me."

  "Your silence speaks volumes."

We have determined that talking about our birth families to our parents is not disloyalty! Thus, we are now at a fork in the road where we must decide what path we will take—the narrow or the wide. We'll see what's involved with both paths in the following chapter.

Two roads diverged in a wood

And I took the one less traveled by
And that has made all the difference.

—ROBERT FROST

CHAPTER fifteen

We Must Give Up Being Pleasers

We're at a fork in the road now and there's a sign pointing in two directions. One part says "Familiar" and the other, "Unknown."

The road called "Familiar" looks appealing because it's broad, smooth, and well-traveled. The other road, "Unknown," is narrow, infested with crabgrass and dandelions, and appears long unused. Ahead is a forest of trees that looks impenetrable.

The road called "Familiar" represents the opinions and feelings of others about what we should say or do in regard to the option of searching for and reuniting with our birth families. "Unknown" is the road that leads straight into our hearts and speaks to us with a still, small voice.

What road will each one of us take? Will we take the familiar road by listening only to the voices of others, possibly ending up with a heart full of bitterness and what-might-have-beens? Or will we take the road of Robert Frost, the less travelled narrow one, and be true to that still, small voice that says, "This is the way; walk in it"?[1]

I am a strong advocate for searching, because I believe that *through the process*, no matter where it leads, we will grow. In grace. In love. In forgiveness. In peace. It's a win/win situation because positive personal growth occurs regardless of the outcome. Every fear must be faced and every stone overturned as we seek clues to our past. This is my opinion, I humbly realize. It is the way I'm wired.

Some of us might not be able to make a literal search, but we can search in other ways in order to connect with our past. For instance, Susan was left on the steps of an orphanage in Romania with only a diaper to her name. She can't obtain any history, but she could still do some searching by visiting her birth land and seeing the orphanage she lived in. Or she could make a "life book," filled with images of her native land.

There comes a time for many when we *know* we want to search. Every time we dream about the possibility, we are pumped! We have gone too far down the adoption road to turn back. What is the driving force behind all that adrenaline?

Our quest for truth

The quest for truth, plain and simple. Truth about ourselves. Truth about what is written on our sealed adoption certificates and hospital records. Truth about how adoption has impacted our lives. Truth about our "other" parents and family out there somewhere. Truth about how our adoptive parents *really* feel about a possible reunion. Truth about what life is all about. Truth about what Truth really is.

Bob Blanchard says, "It really doesn't matter if the outcome of your search is good or not—it's just important to know the truth."

We have this burning desire to know because truth brings freedom. Freedom from the adoption baggage we have carried around for years. Freedom from the paralysis of not being able to be ourselves and know it's okay. Freedom from shallow living and compromise.

Even though we have this wonderful promise of growth and freedom that results from discovering truth, it's scary to embark on the narrow road and, as a result, our search may wax and wane as the years go by. But that's okay.

Laurie says that her search flickered on and off like a light bulb, but beneath the flickering was a steady desire to know the truth.

"It took me a long time to decide to go ahead and begin searching," says Ron Hilliard. "I had actually begun the process about five years earlier only to decide not to proceed. At that point I think I was mostly afraid of what I would find, and especially afraid that if I did find my birth mother, she would not want to have anything to do with me."

Paula Oliver remembers being excited, scared, hopeful, and wary, all at the same time. "Mostly I felt like I was on a treasure hunt."

The risks of searching

Why does the narrow road often feel so scary? Because those ominous woods that lie ahead may be filled with either life-giving redemption or heart-wrenching rejection. Therefore, we must count the cost before we begin to determine if we are willing to expose ourselves to such risk.

Disillusionment

The illusion of many is that if we search and find the long-lost relative and ultimately have a glorious reunion, all adoption-related issues will disappear.

Oops…there's that adoptee fantasy again! Many adoptees in support groups chuckle when another member returns fresh from a reunion.

"Do you still feel adopted?" we all ask.

The answer is always yes, accompanied by a red face!

Feelings of being adopted *don't* go away! Nor should they! Adoption doesn't define us, but it is an event that has impacted us greatly.

Rejection from a birth parent

Another risk of reuniting is rejection from a birth parent, which is common.

"Fear? You betcha!" says Connie Dawson. "When adoptees consider searching (getting what they need), they are faced with huge risks."

Connie's fear was that if her birth family (her birth mother was dead) "rejected" her, and by contacting them she might put her relationship with her adoptive parents at risk, then she would have no one. She would be nowhere.

> I would have seen to my own exile. This is the same fearful space I faced when my birth mother 'sent me away' and I felt that every connection I had was severed. I was like any animal who is born, who is helpless, and whose mother walks off.

Lorraine says that her birth father refuses all responsibility and that opening herself up to a reunion with him would be a crisis waiting to happen. She wouldn't be able to withstand the heartache and rejection.

Fear of not being able to handle the emotions

Another risk we must face is that overwhelming emotion may occur.

Penny Callan Partridge says:

> Many of us don't want to risk having strong feelings, or particular feelings, stirred up. Ultimately, we are probably choosing between one set of feelings and another: the feelings that go along with not knowing versus the feelings that may be stirred up if we choose to try to learn more. But none of these fears is enough to stop the majority of us. The need to know about ourselves, to know our own stories, is just too great.

Adoptive parents may feel hurt

The most pressing concern for Jody Moreen when she contemplated searching was that she would alienate her adoptive parents. Though she had an open, honest, and loving relationship with her adoptive mother, the whole story of her birth and adoption was not a topic ever brought up for discussion. She had always been a very pleasing and compliant child, and desired her parents' approval. Therefore, it was difficult for her to give herself permission as an adult in her thirties to search for the missing pieces of her past. She didn't know how her adoptive parents would interpret her search and was concerned about hurting them in any way.

It took Renee Mills nine months to finally tell her adoptive mother that she had been matched with her birth mother through the International Soundex Reunion Registry. She was terrified of hurting her. She was flying to Florida to meet her birth mother and didn't want to lie to her adoptive mom about her destination. Renee asked her adoptive mother to sit down because she had something very important to tell her. It was then that she began showing pictures of her birth family sent to her by her birth mother. Tears flowed, but at last it was all out in the open. Sometimes she senses her mom getting defensive when she talks about her birth mother, but her mother has encouraged their relationship. Renee's birth mother and adoptive mother have now met each other and both express appreciation for the role the other plays in Renee's life.

The rewards of searching

Obviously, searching entails some significant risks, and each of us must make our own decision. It's our choice to make, and no one else's.

But now on to the good part of searching—the rewards!

Feeling of completeness

"I am complete," says Kasey Hamner. "I know who I am and what I want in life. No more secrets and lies. No more wondering where I got my funny-looking knees or if depression is part of my family history. Knowledge is power, in my opinion."

Phyllis-Anne Munro has gained a much greater sense of wholeness. For years she never believed she could be or deserved to be a mother. After meeting her birth father, for the first time she felt she could parent. "I feel a much greater sense of who I am. What a gift!"

Richard Curtis says that if growth is accomplished through truth and knowledge, then since beginning his search and reunion process, eight years of healing have occurred in his life. The results, he says, are a sense of peace, serenity, and an understanding of where he fits in the universe:

Understanding my adoption experience, has allowed me to bring authenticity to my relationships with family, friends, and others in my life. I no longer hide my thoughts and feelings—the veil of secrecy has been lifted. People now get the real Richard since I've uncovered my past, understand how precious the present is, and perhaps have an idea of where I'm going and who's going with me in the future. Perhaps these are the blessings I can also offer to others.

Self-confidence

"I think that searching was more about finding myself than it was about finding my birth family," says Ron Hilliard:

> The process of finding my birth family led to the realization that "this is who I am." A whole part of me was discovered, and I have found that the process of finding my true identity is still going on. I "found my voice"—I now speak out of a real authenticity because I have a clearer sense of who I am

For Kenny Tucker, meeting both his birth parents was life-changing. "I am more secure in who I am. I feel I can accomplish anything since I waded through the fears of rejection to the other side. I am humbled by the magnitude of it all."

Laurie's search has helped her to accept her beginnings. Before searching she had so much anger about not knowing her past. She found a tombstone at the end of her search for her birth mother but has been able to glean information about her from relatives. As a result, she is better able to accept herself.

A painful past fades

Issie came to the conclusion that she couldn't help the circumstances of her childhood, but that she could still create her own life. She was placed with parents who were dirt poor and tried to poison her mind about her birth parents from day one. "White trash," they called them. Mentally ill. No morals when it came to sex. Issie doesn't know who her father is even though her adoptive parents know and could tell her if they were the least bit loving.

Issie used to be terrified of rejection, but now she is proving that healing has arrived at her heart's doorstep—she is able to "reject her rejection". Her faith assures her that she is loved and cherished, perhaps even more so because of all she's been through.

Increased ability to love and be loved

After Frieda Moore talked with her birth mother, she finally felt like she belonged in her adoptive family. She says the love and acceptance were there all along, but she couldn't receive or give love the way she longed to until she completed her search and reunion. She was finally able to be vulnerable enough to love and let others love her.

Deepened love for adoptive parents

When Jody Moreen found her birth family, both parents were deceased, but she had three living sisters. Not long after a successful reunion with the sisters, her adoptive parents met them and everyone was warm and welcoming.

Jody says:

> The most precious gift my adoptive mother has ever given me was when, unbeknown to me, she bought a bouquet of flowers and suggested we drive to the cemetery to visit my birth mother's grave. We walked silently to the unmarked grave and I wept as my mother gently laid the flowers down at the site. Never in this world have I felt closer to my mother. To think that she would honor my birth mother like this has forever deepened my love for her.

These are just a few of the rewards of surviving the winter of our souls. I can assure you that you will grow tremendously, whether the outcome of your search is positive or painful. Even though my reunion turned sour and I have no relationship with my birth mother whatsoever, I have grown in ways I never dreamed possible. In fact, I believe I have grown more as a result of being rejected!

And so, in light of all the "wins"—some wonderful, some painful—of search and reunion, what choice do we need to make?

Our Choice
To counsel with others but then make our own decisions.

This can feel like a daunting assignment for us because of our deep fears of rejection and abandonment. But be honest with yourself: don't you think it's time someone *really heard* your heart? *You* are that person.

How to begin

- *Make a list of pros and cons about searching.* The only person who needs to be convinced that it is time to search is you. Right now your heart may feel overwhelmed with some of the feelings that our fellow adoptees have discussed. What is needed is an objective look at the whole idea of search and reunion, and a list such as this will help accomplish that purpose.

- *Define in your own words what it means to be true to yourself.* Then go back as far in life as you can remember and list the major decisions you have made. Put a "T" after the ones in which you were true to yourself and your own growth process; put an "X" after the ones in which you weren't. Then review the "X" answers and write about how you could have been true to your process. It certainly might not be too late!

Now that we've considered the risks as well as the rewards of searching, it's time to begin thinking about taking some concrete steps. We'll cover that in the following chapter. We're on the upward swing now in our journey, so hold tight.

Any search for information no matter how 'high' or 'low' the purpose—whether it is baseball statistics or philosophy—is valid because it is a search for truth.

—MONA MCCORMICK

CHAPTER sixteen

Taking Concrete Steps toward Obtaining Our Pre-Adoption History Requires Courage... We Can Do It!

If your list of pros and cons encouraged you to go ahead with your search, this chapter is for you. Nothing is impossible. It may *seem* that way, but you will be surprised at what may show up when you start digging.

Some of you may have much more information to start with than others. Because of the wonderful efforts of the AAC and similar groups, a few states now have open records. Some states also have registries through which birth parents and adoptees can register to let the other person know they are interested in reuniting. Other countries such as Canada and the UK have totally open records.

Others of you may be experiencing an open adoption and have no need to search. You are in direct contact with your birth parents. Let me warn you, however, that as great as open adoption is, it's not the panacea. I have a friend who has experienced an open adoption and she fell apart when she went off to college. The issue of grief remains the same for those of you who know your birth parents because you don't know them in the way that you would have had they chosen to keep and parent you. This is a great loss that needs to be grieved.

The suggestions I make for searching are from my own experience. Each state or country differs in adoption laws and regulations, so my counsel is only a springboard to get you thinking and moving forward with some sense of direction. How sorry I am not to have known about the wonderful resource book on searching by Jayne Askin titled *Search: A Handbook for Adoptees and Birth Parents*. She goes into much more detail than I can here.

Concrete steps for searching

Based on my experience, here are some steps to take in searching for your birth parents, in logical sequence.

Find out if your state/country has an adoption registry

Some states have adoption registries through which both birth parents and adoptees can file a document stating that they would like contact. Contact your county courthouse for this information.

Contact the adoption agency

Mine was a private adoption, so I didn't have the resource of an adoption agency, but the majority of adoptees do. Were you adopted through an agency, or were you a ward of the state? Whatever the case, request in writing that they provide names of birth parents for you...or any clues they may possess.

If you don't have your birth mother's name, ask the current social worker at the agency through which you were adopted. A friend of mine did this and every time they chatted, the social worker revealed another bit of information. In time, my friend had the name.

I am not implying that you manipulate the social worker, but "the squeaky wheel gets the grease." There is nothing wrong with consistent contact. Remember, you have the moral right to know your history.

Request a Non-Identifying Information form from your county of birth

The next thing would be to contact the probate judge in the county where you were born (if you know it), and request the Non-Identifying Information form. This will not give names of birth parents but will give details such as occupations, ages of parents at your birth, and where you come in the order of children born to your mother.

This can be a somewhat frustrating method for obtaining information, but at least it's a start, and you will likely not have to pay for this information.

Request your original birth certificate from the state health department

The majority of US adoptees have "amended" birth certificates, with the names of adoptive parents listed in the parent category.

When you write to the state health department of your birth state requesting your original birth certificate, you may be denied outright, funneled to another office, or simply receive another amended certificate.

Does that make you as mad as it does me? Jayne Askin quotes an individual who echoes my sentiments, and possibly yours:

> We are not separate or different than those born with a heritage they have always had knowledge of…and the freedom to investigate further if they so choose. Being denied information concerning myself that is not denied a non-adoptee is degrading and cruel…what an invasion of humanity…to close up a human life as a vault somewhere and say, "You may not know about yourself—you have not the right to even ask…your anxieties are neurotic, your curiosity unnatural."[1]

I wrote to the state department of health and requested my birth certificate under the only name I had—the one my adoptive parents gave me (not "Baby X," as the hospital nurses had "named" me). This was a different document than my dad had given me. His was an adoption certificate. What I was seeking was my *original* birth certificate. Why did I want it even though I already knew my parents' names? Because I wanted proof that what was written on Dad's certificate was the truth. In addition, I wanted with all my heart to break the secrecy. I hate secrecy!

In my letter I didn't say that I was adopted. I didn't lie in any way; I simply asked for what any other citizen has a legal right to obtain. Within weeks I had my original birth certificate in my hands…and I didn't break the law!

You may want to try this if your circumstances are similar.

Contact the hospital for birth records

Next, make a stop at the hospital where you were born. If you can't travel there, write a letter requesting your birth information. Again, don't use the "A" word—"adoptee"!

When I contacted the hospital where I was born, I began a long battle with the superintendent of records for my birth records, which I will tell you about it in more detail in the next chapter.

Some hospitals readily release records and some remain rigidly closed, like the one where I was born.

Ask your physician to request release of hospital records

My next line of attack was to ask my current physician if he would write a letter requesting hospital records, which he did. He requested not only my birth records, but also those of my birth mother.

Asking for these doesn't require a medical emergency. An emotional hurt needs to be resolved, and if your physician won't write a letter for you, maybe it's time to find another physician.

Conduct your own research at the state library

Your next step may be to visit the state library in your birth state. The library contains city directories from the past, which can be amazing resources. For example, in the 1940s when I was born, they contained not only people's names and addresses, but also their occupation and other details. These are even more pieces you can put in your puzzle.

Usually you'll find librarians at such a facility who specialize in genealogy and who are more than eager to help you find information. You can even say you're an adoptee without discrimination! Don't be afraid to ask these professionals for assistance.

Hire an adoption professional

Sometimes it's difficult to find someone who won't charge an arm and a leg to do a birth parent search. But I was lucky. I learned of a professional in a town near my place of birth and I was able to hire her for $100. I don't suppose you'll find anyone that inexpensive nowadays, but it's an option well worth considering if you're running into roadblocks in your search, or simply want an experienced guide throughout this process.

If you are having difficulty finding a professional, contact adoption support groups in your birth locale and ask who they would recommend. They usually know the possibilities better than anyone.

Comb death records on ancestry.com

The professional I worked with believed that we would be able to narrow down our search further by seeing which of the people I found in the library's city directories were already deceased. We went to the local branch of the Church of Jesus Christ of Latter-Day Saints, which had the most extensive death records in the US. We went through the microfiche and found several possibilities whom my guide believed could be my grandfather and grandmother.

Visit the state health department

The last stop for me was to the state health department, where we obtained death certificates of the people who may have been my grandparents. Within an hour we had identified my grandfather's certificate, which contained valuable information such as the funeral home that took care of the arrangements for his burial.

You will have to pay a fee and fill out a form for each death certificate you order. We ordered more than needed, but it narrowed down the search to the final clue.

Contact the funeral home for survivors

The name of the funeral home where arrangements were made listed all survivors by name and address. This is a part of my story I'm not proud of, but I have to declare complete ignorance about the approach my adoption worker took with the funeral director. When we found the information about the funeral home, she just told me to go home and wait for her call. Never did it enter my mind whether or not what she was doing was ethical. I think she introduced herself as a family friend. In other words, she lied. But the funeral director was very cooperative and had no problem in giving names and phone numbers of family members who were still living at the time of my grandfather's death—including his daughter, my birth mother.

While I wouldn't recommend the "little white lie" approach my adoption worker took, the funeral director might still be an excellent resource. Who knows, if you or your adoption worker approach him in complete honesty and he gives the information, great! At least you will have a clean conscience about it all and you will obtain facts that any other citizen has every right to know!

Whether we are taking our first step toward uncovering our pre-adoption history or our tenth, we need courage. Courage to face our past history, whether the details are pleasant or painful. Courage to stand up for our rights, even if we have to haul someone to court. Courage to fight for the unsealing of records. Courage to keep on keeping on when treated like an errant child. And courage to believe that this is all going to be worth it in the end.

I was terrified all those years ago when I began my feeble attempts at searching. But looking back I can say confidently from my experience that courage comes when we need it.

The late Corrie ten Boom, once a Nazi prisoner of war, asked her father when she was young how she would ever have the courage to face death. Her father's answer was simple. He said something like this: "Corrie, when do I give you your ticket to get on the train?"

"Well, just before I get on, Papa," she said.

"That's the way it is when you die," her papa told her. "You will have the courage when you need it."[2]

That's the way it will be for us as we take one concrete step after another.

Our Choice

To take our first or next step toward obtaining our birth certificates, medical records, and/or other information about our birth families.

I still remember when I scratched out a letter to the probate judge in pencil on simple notebook paper. Bob and I were vacationing in northern Michigan. The rest of the family was out on the beach, but that flame for truth had been ignited within me so that even the beach I loved didn't seem as inviting as taking my first concrete step toward gaining information about my past.

I wish you the best as you begin your search! Remember that you will grow no matter what the outcome. So step forward with confidence.

How to begin

- *Obtain the name of the probate judge in your birth county.*
  Call the city offices and ask for the name and address
  so that you can begin that first letter requesting a Non-
  Identifying Information form. Ask about adoption
  support groups. When you call the city offices, ask for
  information about support groups in the area where you
  were born.

- *Consider joining Ancestry.com.* Fabulous and fascinating
  finds there.

- *Enter "adoption reunion, adoptee search" in your search
  engine.* Follow until you find something helpful.

- *Find an all-adoptee online group for support.* Make sure it
  is safe and for adoptees only.

- *Get coaching.* My husband, Bob, is a "Life-Coach." He
  helps people find their life purpose through personality
  testing and profiles. Begin your search in your own
  country and see what you can come up with. Ask
  associations of coaches to provide you with references
  of people that will give you honest feedback. Google and
  investigate your options.

As we begin to take concrete steps, at times we will feel
overwhelmed with emotion. Fear. Confusion. Frustration.
Disappointment. Exhilaration. In fact, you may be feeling that
way right now, after reading this chapter. Perhaps you haven't
begun your search and the whole thing sounds incredibly
intimidating.

Remember, we're on a path toward life transformation.
It's one step at a time. When we are feeling overwhelmed, it is
time to pull back a little and be gentle with ourselves. We'll talk
about that next.

Tears pour from my eyes, screaming out for someone who is not there to embrace me. I long for a recess from life's complexity.

—CELTIC STAR

CHAPTER seventeen

When We Feel Overwhelmed We Must Be Gentle with Ourselves

Sometimes, it's hard to understand why things happen the way they do. When I was writing the first edition of this book, I stared at the title of this chapter for hours, wondering what to write.

Then I went to the mailbox and found a letter from the probate judge's office of the county where I was born, saying that there was no more they could do in regard to releasing my birth records from the hospital. My "overwhelm level" hit an all-time high!

Let me back up a few years and you may understand why.

The battle for my records had been going on for *twelve* years. After going through all the steps in the previous chapter, I went to the hospital *again*, explaining how important authentic birth information is for an adoptee. I hoped that perhaps a little education about adoption would help the superintendent soften her position.

She kindly invited me to go down into the hospital basement where the records were stored. My heart was beating like a drum! Maybe she was going to have a little compassion and relent. Why else would she have gone to the trouble of taking me there?

She left me at the door to the records vault and went to look for my file. After a few minutes she returned and said that my records were there but that I couldn't see them. "Confidentiality," she said, dangling the bait and then taking it away.

My body began shaking with deep sobs as she stood at a distance, like a marble statue. She walked away as I wept.

Not long afterward my husband called her and explained the importance of having my records. She pulled them out of my file, read them to herself, and announced to Bob that there was *absolutely nothing significant* about the birth. Why would I want such records so badly? (*Silly little adoptee!*)

I finally hired a lawyer who wrote an "ex parte order." The judge replied that there was no reason why I shouldn't be treated like any other person in regard to confidentiality provisions of the law, since I already had my original birth certificate and had been reunited with my birth mother. The hospital superintendent's response was that "this will be the last we would hear of this" and that I could *not* have my records.

A few weeks before writing this chapter I wrote to the probate judge saying that I believed the superintendent was in contempt of court. The reply was that "they had done all they could for me." That was the letter I received while trying to write this chapter.

I remembered Jayne Askin's words about our rights as adoptees:

> Under the American system of government, citizens (either as individuals or organized into groups pursuing defined interests) can raise a challenge to any federal, state, or local statute or administrative policy affecting them that appears inconsistent with the guarantees contained in the Constitution of the United States.[1]

I got all fired up, thinking I could now appeal to the state.

But then a new thought dawned on me. Why? Was it *really* birth information I wanted? Was it *really* to be treated fairly by the law?

No, I think there was much more to it. A big part of my stance by this point was about control. My birth mother had the final word about sending me away, and I was determined not to let her have the *last* say.

Even as I wrote this chapter I could feel another layer of rage that I never knew was there. I guess my next step of growth must be more forgiveness. We'll talk about that in a later chapter. For now, it helps me to know that I'm not the only one who has felt overwhelmed somewhere along the way in the process of dealing with adoption-related loss and searching for connections to my past.

Why are we overwhelmed at times?

At times we can get absolutely crazy and obsessed over searching. Once we've turned onto the "narrow road," all we can think about is what lies ahead. Sheila Rounds says, "When you are searching and you keep hitting roadblocks, it's exhaustingly painful."

Sharon McGowan feels overwhelmed several times a year and throws herself a pity party. She also tries to get moving—to do something…anything—so that she can feel more in control of the uncontrollable.

Oh, the uncontrollable. How we adoptees hate that old feeling of having no control!

Lack of information

Wanting to proceed with searching but having absolutely no information to go on can be incredibly frustrating.

Laurie spends endless hours at the computer or looking over the information she does have. Often it seems impossible to her to make any progress.

Don't give up, Laurie! You are growing even though you're frustrated. Remember that reunion is not the panacea…the process is.

Richard Curtis is also furious about his time spent researching, and frustrated that adult adoptees are still being treated like children. He laments the fact that those who were adopted many years ago usually don't have the legal advantages of younger adoptees.

Concern for our children and/ or grandchildren

Whenever my children or grandchildren have health problems, I always feel angry that I know only half my history. None of my descendants will ever know their complete health histories.

Derek Jeske has similar feelings. There is always that unknown factor, which scares him, especially when it comes to having children. To not know if there are any health-related issues in his background and then to have children and wonder if he's passing along any diseases is unsettling for him.

Society's view of adoptees

Up until recently, I dare say that 99 percent of American media reports demonstrate ignorance and denial concerning adoptions and adoptees. For example, when someone commits a heinous crime and he *just happens* to be an adoptee, the press snatches it up and makes sure that the public knows that the murderer was adopted.

How often do we hear about all the highly successful people who were adopted, such as Nancy Reagan, Gerald Ford, Dave Thomas, and Melissa Gilbert? The media doesn't say, "Adopted President Gerald Ford"! On Wendy's commercials, the late fast-food chain founder didn't say, "Hi, I'm adopted Dave Thomas." Come on, now!

Jodi Strathman agrees that many media stories associate adoptees with criminal acts. She says, "Let's get real…the majority of adoptees are not mentally ill or murderers!"

The media is starting to come around. You will be surprised as you watch how television programs, both now and in years to come, weave in the topic of adoption.

Stigma

The warped views of society in general naturally spill over to individuals in our lives. Karen says,

> I'm tired of having the feelings that are so close to my heart be something that makes others uncomfortable. Most people don't want to know about it. As soon as you bring it up, you've got "the Plague." It's very hard to cope when very few people have compassion for the most difficult challenge in my life.

Teresa Armor, a transracial adoptee, says that the cultural factor is definitely involved in stigma. She says answering questions about her adoption from ignorant yet well-meaning people can feel a little overwhelming. In response, she tries to educate whoever is asking, and show them why the difference they observe in appearance and personalities within her family is not because of their mixed culture, but because of the uniqueness of every individual.

Discouragement

Ron Hilliard says that there are times when he just wishes he were "normal"! As he has become aware of how early-life loss has impacted him, he sometimes gets discouraged. He says that it seems like he keeps dealing with the same adoption issues over and over again, with no permanent relief:

> I somehow believe that I should get over it, or move beyond it, and when I find I haven't it's discouraging and frustrating. I feel as though there is something wrong with me for still being impacted by the issues. I feel overwhelmed about adoption in the midst of relationships. I guess I believe that some of my relationship struggles wouldn't be going on if I weren't adopted. And it takes a lot of energy to work through the issues I have related to adoption.

Whenever Sharon McGowan sees a baby on television whose parents are thrilled about its arrival, or a baby who's not wanted, she becomes a baby emotionally for a few minutes and is overwhelmed with pain, loneliness, and hopelessness.

These comments remind me of a story I once heard. It was advertised that the Devil was going to put his tools up for sale. On the day of the sale, they were marked for public inspection, each·with a sale price. The tools were hatred, envy, jealousy, deceit, and pride. Apart from the rest was a very harmless looking tool, very well worn, but expensively priced. "What is the name of this tool?" asked one of the purchasers. "Ah," said the Devil, "that is discouragement." When asked why he priced it so high, he said, "Oh, because it's more useful to me than all the others. I can pry open and get into a man's heart with that when I can't get near him with any other tool. And once I'm inside, I can do with him whatever I choose. It's badly worn because I use it on almost everyone, but few people know that it belongs to me."[2]

Uncooperative birth mothers

Something else that can feel overwhelming to adult adoptees is uncooperative birth mothers.

Cheri Manternach's birth mother wants nothing to do with her after forty-one years, and Cheri is experiencing an illness that is hereditary. Her mother won't give her even the most basic medical information about her family of origin:

> Some years ago, I woke up on a hospital gurney after having a grand mal seizure. Of course, the first thought that came to mind was, I wonder if this is hereditary. At this point my mother would not talk to me and so my husband called. She just laughed at my request for medical information like it was a joke and expressed disapproval of the contact for such an "insignificant" matter.

Overextending ourselves for others

Another avenue that can lead to feelings of no control is when we become overactive in trying to help others. We try to pour out to others from an empty pitcher and it just doesn't work.

Just ask Kenny Tucker. He often feels overwhelmed by his activism activities and helping other adoptees search.

Dawn Saphir says:

> At first I couldn't get enough information, I couldn't meet enough adoptees, and I certainly couldn't learn enough

about Korea, my birth country. As I have gotten older, I have been overwhelmed with feeling *obligated* to do this work and confront these issues to help others.

Many of us have chosen to go back into the system that has injured us in hopes of helping others. Phyllis-Anne Munro works in the foster care system, which triggers her own issues at times. She does the best she can but sometimes she just comes home and cries, while at other times feels rage about the injustice she continues to see.

So what do we do when we feel overwhelmed? To put it simply: we nurture ourselves.

How we nurture ourselves

Dr. Paul Brand, a missionary physician in India who has worked with children with clubbed feet, learned that if he could draw the child's attention to an urgent need, such as intense hunger, the deep satisfaction of having that need met would set up a barrier for pain and he could easily correct the clubbed feet.

The child's mother was to refrain from nursing until the examination. When the time came and she sat opposite Dr. Brand, laid her child across her knees, and opened her sari, her breasts were swollen with milk. As the child sucked greedily at her breast, Dr. Brand removed the old splint and washed the foot, then began to move it around "to test the range of movement." Sometimes the child would turn its eyes toward him and frown, but eating was the overwhelming priority. If the child quit nursing in order to yell, that meant Dr. Brand had gone too far and forced the foot into a position that would put tissue under too much stress. At the first cry of protest, doctor and mother would have to wait, unwrap the plaster, and start over with a new bandage while the child went back to the breast. Dr. Brand says:

If we crossed the pain barrier, even though we could see no obvious injury, swelling and stiffness would later appear. Using this technique we got dramatic results of total correction without resorting to surgery. The correcting influence had to be both gentle and persistent.[3]

Just like Dr. Brand's patients, our emotional "feet" often feel clubbed by adoption-related issues. If we are not gentle with ourselves when feeling overwhelmed, we may cross our own pain barriers and get into trouble emotionally.

But how can we be gentle with ourselves? We do it well with others, but often fall short of giving ourselves the gift. Here are some ideas from fellow adoptees.

Rely on a good support system

Dirck Brown relies on prayer and key people, especially his wife Molly and his Episcopal priest:

It also helped to create the Post Adoption Center for Education and Research (PACER) and have almost weekly sessions of our triad support group—a powerful experience to be able to share your joys and frustrations with others facing the same issues.

Dirck also uses PACER to educate professionals and others about the long-term issues related to adoption that the public generally discounts.

Joy Budensiek says God brought people into her life who have given of themselves by sharing their own joy and pain. As a result, she can grow emotionally and blend into life rather than be consumed by her own broken heart.

Soak in unconditional love

"Part of nurturing myself is simply allowing myself not to be perfect," says Ron Hilliard. "To realize that I am a work in progress and to not fall into believing that being relinquished is something to 'get over.' This is who I am, and it is okay to be who I am."

What a comfort. We can choose to allow ourselves to feel what we feel. We're not being graded!

Phyllis-Anne Munro's husband makes her feel treasured and safe by letting her be in whatever emotional space she is and loving her unconditionally. Their relationship has healed some very deep wounds she has carried for years.

Learn how to have fun

One of my therapists told me years ago that I needed to learn to have fun—that, she said, is the final step of healing.

I used to love to ice skate as a child, and I was actually pretty good! I dreamed of being a famous figure skater when I grew up. I remember Dad coming to watch me practice almost every night. He'd sit out in the cold on a bench and watch with pride as I did figure-eights on the ice.

Maybe that early experience with Dad has something to do with why I love to roller blade. I know it has a direct correlation to my birth mother—she was named the Ice Skating Queen in the town where she grew up.

I bought myself a pair of blades a few years ago, and when I'm out there swirling through the streets, listening to my favorite music on my iPod, adoption is the furthest thing from my mind.

Often Bob and I go to a big corporation's parking lot after hours, just before the sun goes down. (I've converted him into roller blading too!) I not only swirl through the lot, but I sing at the top of my lungs. I am a terrible singer...but I don't even care!

And so, what life-transforming choice can we make when we feel overwhelmed by issues related to being adopted?

Our Choice

To accept our limits and nurture ourselves.

Don't you feel a little relieved, knowing that we have similar limitations and irritations? After we have learned to accept our limits, we can nurture ourselves by one or all of the following.

How to begin

- *Get a massage.* Especially if you've never had one before! It is a relaxing experience and takes away all the stress you are carrying in your body.

- *Listen to soothing music before going to sleep.* I started doing this when I was far away from home, in China, during the 9/11 crisis. It brought such comfort that I have continued the practice ever since. Try lying in bed, covered up, and let the music relax you.

- *Read something inspiring.* For me, this is most often my Bible. I love the new paraphrased versions that have come out lately, especially *The Message*, by Eugene Peterson.

Now that you're all nurtured, it's time to turn again to a subject nobody likes to talk about—rejection.

Sorrow is a kind of rust of the soul, which every new idea contributes in its passage to scour away. It is the putrefaction of stagnant life, and is remedied by exercise and motion.

—SAMUEL JOHNSON

CHAPTER eighteen

Rejection Might Be Part of Your Adoptee "Rite of Passage"

Rejection. Just the sound of the word sends chills up my spine!

Rejection is the dark side of the search and reunion process. The agonizing side. The side that is rarely, if ever, talked about. The side that the media never covers.

It is also part of our adoptee "rite of passage" into a healthier, more fulfilling life. So, don't despair, my friends, if you are experiencing this right now. You *will* get through it.

How many of us are rejected? Statistics, as for most aspects of adoption, are sadly non-existent. While many claim that only a minority of adoptees are rejected by a birth relative at reunion, during the years I have been researching and talking with other adoptees, however, I have found rejection to be rampant and common.

Why do birth relatives reject some of us? Does our physical appearance remind our birth mothers of our fathers, whom they have no positive feelings for? Does seeing us trigger issues in them that they have never dealt with? Are they emotionally and mentally unbalanced? Or are they just downright mean?

What does it mean to be rejected and how does it feel? My dictionary gives us a good start on understanding its basic message: "Refusing to have, take, or act upon. To refuse to accept a person. To rebuff. To throw away or discard as useless or unsatisfactory. To cast out or eject. Something rejected as an imperfect article."[1]

Ron Nydam, Ph.D., gives a vivid illustration from a client's encounter with his birth mother. She told her son: "If you want answers, see a psychiatrist; if you want a companion, get a dog."[2]

I will never forget when I was reeling from my birth mother's rejection. While attending my first AAC, a man at one of the book tables asked me to tell him my story. I got to the part where I was going to say, "All I wanted was for her to say the words 'I love you,'" and I lost it. He looked me straight in the eyes and said, "It really hurts, doesn't it?" I knew by the tone of his voice that this wasn't some platitude—it came from his heart. This dear man took me into the lobby of the hotel and told me how he had experienced the same rejection from his birth mother years ago. Still, after all that time, he wept.

As I personally became aware of this fear of being forgotten and shared it with the adoptees in my support group, eyes welled with tears and you could have heard a pin drop.

Karen says that her birth mother rejected her "right out of the gate." She didn't even give Karen the dignity of getting to know her first before making up her mind. Karen was her dirty secret and she couldn't stand the thought of others knowing.

She told her that her mother (Karen's grandmother) would also reject her.

As Karen reflects on the rejection, she says:

> She didn't just reject me—she wanted nothing to do with my son, her own grandson! When I found her, my son wasn't even one year old, a beautiful baby. How could she reject him? The only time I met her she reviewed pictures I had brought of him with detachment and terse comments.

When birth siblings learn that a parent conceived an unknown child, their reaction may be to reject us as well.

Laurie's birth half-sister found it difficult to speak with her since she was told that Laurie was her half-sister. Laurie, like Karen, was her birth mother's secret. Laurie has tried to make contact, but her birth mother wants nothing to do with her. She is hoping that one day she will speak to her, or that at least she will eventually develop a relationship with her half-sister.

Richard Curtis says:

> Even though I have not been overtly rejected by birth relatives, I have the feeling that I'm being ignored or at least overlooked by family members who just don't know what to do with me. Both of my birth parents were deceased when I finally conducted my search and so my 'reunions' have been with siblings and cousins. That being the case, after the initial shock and curiosity of discovering a secret birth relative, most members of both families have relegated me to receiving a card at Christmas or an occasional email. At first I tried to take the initiative and keep in contact, especially with my siblings; but I've gotten little response.

Okay, that's enough. We know the realities of rejection. Let's not stay there unless we are currently experiencing it. Then, fellow adoptee hurt words are validating. But for the rest of us, let's move on, okay?

If we've received hostile responses from birth relatives, how do we usually react?

We isolate ourselves

Isolation and rejection partner to silence us. We are frozen in fear and don't want another soul to know our experience. We feel we have been branded for life.

We *do* need isolation from the rejecting birth relatives, but *not* from fellow adoptees who have had similar experiences. In their company we can find a *good* kind of isolation, where we experience protection, comfort, strength, validation, and healing.

After I shared my fear of being forgotten with the adoptees in my support group, I thought about it a lot in the days to come. Aren't we as rejected adoptees a little like prisoners of war? Aren't we missing in action in many ways?

While studying the subject of being forgotten, I saw a poster-sized reproduction of a US commemorative stamp. The poster depicted an army dog tag on a chain, inscribed with the words, "MIA and POW—NEVER FORGOTTEN." These two words grabbed my attention—NEVER FORGOTTEN.

My sweet husband purchased a gold ID bracelet with a chain like a dog tag. On one side I had the jeweler inscribe "Baby X." On the other side were the words "Never forgotten."

The message behind their words

Again, here it is so helpful for us to take a deep breath and think about the psychological dynamic of projection. All the rejecting person can see is themselves. So, when they are saying rotten things about us, what are they really doing? They're telling us how they feel about themselves. How freeing this is!

Let's take some examples:

- "I can tell you are in therapy." (I need to be in therapy.)

- "I knew I couldn't trust you." (I can't trust myself.)

- "You are a secret in the family." (I have a secret I've kept from my family.)

- "You remind me of your rapist birth father." (I can't get my rapist out of my mind.)

- "You aren't important to me." (I am not important.)

- "You are disposable." (I am disposable.)

Our rite of passage into a balanced, healthy life

Of all the things I've learned lately about our adoptee journey, the concept of the adoptee's rite of passage is the most exciting. Listen to this story and then we'll draw parallels to our own experiences.

A young American Indian man was about to go through the rite of passage into manhood. Prior to this event, he was prepared to defend himself in every way. On the day of the rite, he was blindfolded and led, gun in hand, into a dark forest and left alone overnight. The blindfold remained all night.

During the night, whenever the wind blew a leaf or an animal scurried through the underbrush, he was sure it was a wild animal seeking to devour him. He was terrified. When morning dawned he removed his blindfold and saw a path leading off to his right. He thought he saw someone at the end of the path. As he contemplated the figure, he realized that it was his father, aimed and ready to shoot anything or anyone that would hurt his son.[3]

Lies and truth about rejection

There is always an end to the dark night of our experience. Many of us might have believed that we'll always be in the darkness and shame of rejection. Like our anger issues, we may easily believe:

- *"There must be something wrong with me or he/she wouldn't reject me. This is shame."* I bet you anything, my friend, after you've done all your searching and reunion "work," that you'll find it's not about you. It's about the dysfunction of the person who rejected you.

- *"Something I did or said, 'made' him/her/them reject me."* We don't have that kind of power! No one does. We all make choices. The rejecting person's choice was totally his/hers.

- *"I'll never get over this hurt."* There's our black-and-white thinking. We will always have memories of the hurt, but the shame, the stinging shame, will fade in time. I promise you. Like the American Indian teen, there will come a day when the sun rises and you realize you were never alone...that's why we need one another. Those fellow-adoptee friendships are vital!

We need to get over ourselves

I believe, as a fellow adoptee friend to you, that I can speak frankly, more so than anyone else. Okay, here we go!

Yes, we need to quit throwing pity parties, focusing on past hurts, licking our wounds, and accept a "new template" for our future life.

Rejection does NOT define us, friends.

We are amazing people. We have survived pre-adoption trauma that's unbelievable. We are survivors…now we need to step into that role with confidence.

Think back to the American Indian teen. Of course, many sounds, movements around him, darkness and all kinds of scary stuff. But he trusted in everything his father had built into him, and every character quality came to fruition during the night. He felt feelings but had the strength from his father's training to not give into fear.

That's you, friend.

Stand strong. Stand tall. You are amazing.

Our Choice

To reject our rejection and not let it define us.

How to begin

- *Journal, journal, journal.* Journaling provides a place for you to pour out your innermost thoughts and feelings.

- *Describe your "adoptee rite of passage."* Where are you in the process? Draw a timeline.

- *Check out this online group: all-adoptees@yahoogroups. com.* We are there for you and there is no reason for isolation.

- *Get a memento.* Like my ID bracelet, to remind you of the day you rejected the rejection(s).

The biggest "take away" for this chapter is—don't do it alone! If you don't know fellow-adoptee friends, contact me. I know adoptees from all over the world who support one another through this "rite of passage."

Home is the place where, when you have to go there, they have to take you in.

—ROBERT FROST

CHAPTER nineteen

The Word "Rejection" May Not Be in the Vocabularies of Other Birth Relatives!

Once, while attending an adoption support group meeting, I heard a statement I'd never heard before: "If your birth mother rejects you, it doesn't mean that the *rest* of your family will."

As I thought about that comment, I concluded that the same blood that pulses through their veins pulses through mine. It was high time to start claiming my birthright.

A few months later I received a call. "Is this Sharon Lee Eldridge?" a woman whispered.

I paused, for no one *ever* calls me Sharon Lee—except when I was a kid and got into trouble.

After acknowledging that I was indeed Sharon Lee, she introduced herself as my birth cousin, Sharon, from Bay City, Michigan. After giving me a few basic facts about our family, I realized that she was reaching out in love. We talked for at least two hours as she gave me her perspective of the family, specifically my birth mother. My cousin had heard about me through "the family grapevine" after I had been rejected by my birth mother. She contacted me out of pure love, hoping that she could restore to me some of the feelings of belonging to my birth family. She told me during our phone call that she wished she could have known me sooner so that she could have warned me prior to meeting my mother about her history of negative behavior.

One week later I received a package from her with black-and-white matted photos of my birth family, going all the way back to the 1800s. As I looked at the faces of my relatives I felt like a little child peering from outside a window on a cold, wintry night, watching a happy family around the fire. After carefully examining the photos I saw no resemblance and concluded that I must look like my birth father, whoever he is or was.

One of Sharon's hobbies is investigating and recording our family's genealogy. She sent me a notebook filled with pages detailing each generation—dates of birth, how many children, where and when they died and were buried. She also sent a thick book written by a distant relative that contained a detailed description of who belonged to whom. When I came to the part about my birth mother and supposed father, there was no mention of me. None. As far as the rest of the family was concerned, I didn't exist.

Sharon must have anticipated the effect that would have on me, so she inked in my name where it should have appeared. We were reunited soon afterward, and a close friendship developed between the two of us over the years.

Claiming my birthright

Because of that positive experience with Sharon, I reflected once more on the statement I had heard at the support group meeting and concluded that it must be true, so I continued my search for other relatives.

Reaching out

I learned from my cousin that we had an aunt living in Michigan, my birth mother's older sister, who was dying of cancer. I decided to contact her via letter.

> Dear Barbara,
>
> You don't know me but I am the first-born child of your sister Marjorie Elizabeth that she gave up for adoption in 1945. A few years ago we had a reunion but unfortunately have no relationship now. I have come to realize that not only is she my birth family, but you and many others are as well. It would be such a joy to meet you. I don't want anything from you—just a chance to meet you face to face. Would you be interested?
>
> Best regards,
>
> Sherrie Eldridge

Well, when my birth mother found out that I had contacted her sister, she went ballistic, which was no surprise. Regardless, my aunt invited my husband and me to visit her in Michigan. We sat together for an hour as she shared memories of the family. Before Bob and I left, my Aunt Barbara struggled out of her Lazy Boy, oxygen tank in tow, walked into the dining room, and carried out a beautiful china bowl, laced in gold leaf. "This was your grandmother's," she said. "I know if she were here she would want you to have it."

After photos and hugs we said goodbye. That was the first and last time I would see her, for she died a few months later. However, the contact with her set off a chain of events that would open more doors in the future.

A welcome surprise

A few years later I got an email that didn't make much sense. It said, "So, you've written a book! Congratulations and welcome to the family."

Welcome to the family? I thought. Who is this, anyway? Is it a fellow author congratulating me on the publication of my book? I didn't reply because I didn't know what to say.

A week later I got a phone call from a woman who asked, "Hello, is this Sherrie Eldridge? The Sherrie Eldridge who wrote *Twenty Things Adopted Kids Wish Their Adoptive Parents Knew*"?

"Yes," I replied, thinking it was a call from someone who had read my book.

"This is your Aunt Marge—I'm the wife of your Uncle Dave from Nashville! Did you get our email?"

"What email?"

"The one that said, 'Welcome to the family!'"

"Oh my goodness!" I gasped. "I had *no* idea that it was from *my* family! Thank you for following through with a telephone call! I would have never put two and two together."

"We thought maybe that was the case so we decided to pick up the phone and call."

After a few minutes of chatting Aunt Marge asked if I would like to talk to my Uncle Dave. *What would he say to me?*

I wondered, suddenly nervous. *Would he reject me like his sister (my mother) had?*

A friendly, jovial voice boomed through the phone lines and for the next forty minutes he relayed fascinating things about my birth family:

> Your great-grandfather and your grandfather were US Coast Guard Lighthouse Keepers on the Great Lakes from the mid-1800s through the mid-1900s. I even lived in one of the lighthouses. Your grandfather carved miniature ships, and one of them was bought by Henry Ford and now is in the museum in Detroit. It's too bad your grandparents didn't know you. They would have loved you and been so proud of you.

Blessings from buffetings

A few months later Bob and I met my aunt and uncle in southern Indiana where they were vacationing. Over a leisurely dinner they showered us with family stories and gifts that once belonged to my grandparents.

Afterward, Bob and I climbed into the back seat of Uncle Dave's shiny yellow Cadillac, and as he pulled into the hotel parking lot he turned up the radio and the old gospel song "How Great Thou Art" filled the air. I got a *huge* lump in my throat. We exchanged hugs and said good night at the elevator.

"Can you believe it?" I said to Bob, leaning my head on his shoulder as tears dripped down his shirt. He hugged me close and said, "It's pretty awesome, isn't it? God really does bring blessings from buffetings."

The next morning when we were walking to the parking lot to say goodbye, Uncle Dave put his arm around me and said, "Sherrie, I love you, and don't you *ever* forget that you're a Clark!"

I choked back the tears, for that was something I had never heard. Something deep down inside me was healed. At last I felt connected and like I belonged!

Since that time I correspond often with my aunt and uncle via email or phone. When I turn on my computer and open a message from Uncle Dave, he always says, "Hello, beautiful! Top of the morning to you and Bob!"

Uncle Dave began connecting me with other family members—two cousins, Sally and Larry. Sally invited us to her home to meet her and her brother, and when we got to her doorstep she swung the door wide open and *ran* to give me a hug. The three of us compared physical features and decided we share the same nose. She gave me a pine cone Christmas tree that my grandmother made years ago that was sitting on my dining room table as I wrote this chapter.

Larry sent me two videos of the family from the time he was a child. I got to see my grandma and grandpa as they really were. Not just black-and-white lifeless photos, but *real* people! How strange to think that my life was unfolding just a four-hour drive from these people who were my family but knew nothing about me.

Discovering my roots

The following autumn Bob and I met Uncle Dave and Aunt Marge for the Michigan Lighthouse Tour and made a whirlwind trip to the Upper Peninsula to see the lighthouse in Brimley, where Uncle Dave once lived as a child. He kept saying, "Sherrie, how many women your age can say that their great-grandfather and grandfather were lighthouse keepers? You have a very special heritage. You are one of us, you know. You can't disown us!"

Sacred steps

As we climbed the same steel, mesh spiral stairway of the Brimley lighthouse that my grandfathers walked every day, generations ago, each step seemed sacred. Silently we gazed upon majestic Lake Superior and the multi-colored fall leaves on the shores of Canada. Uncle Dave told of his childhood experiences to other tourists in the room that once was his. I listened with pride to my sweetheart of an uncle.

Visiting the cemetery

We headed toward Cheboygan where I met two other cousins and saw the old homestead where my birth mother and family had lived. We also visited the gravesite of my grandparents. Prior to going, I asked Uncle Dave to take me to the florist to buy flowers for their graves.

As we approached the headstone, Uncle Dave said, "There it is. That's where your grandparents are buried, Sherrie." We exited the car in silence and I took a few steps forward, bent down, and placed two red carnations and baby's breath on their graves. Tears ran down my cheeks as I stared at the stone.

"They would have loved you so much," Uncle Dave kept saying. "They would have been so proud of you, Sherrie."

His words sunk into my soul, reaching down to every wound that had been inflicted by my birth mother. I felt like I was being bathed in love.

"I wish I could have known them," I said, as Bob held me close.

Three generations connect

A few months later Uncle Dave and Aunt Marge came to visit us in Indianapolis to celebrate Aunt Marge's and my birthdays and also to meet our daughters, their husbands, and our four grandchildren.

At the restaurant that night, as my beautiful adult daughters came through the door and Uncle Dave swept them up in big hugs, I couldn't hold back any longer. I lost it! To think that this was the *first time* my children and grandchildren had ever touched the skin of a blood relative other than me—well, it was more than I could take in.

A story that keeps unfolding

My heart swells as I reflect on all the love my extended birth family has showered on me. Each one of them, in his or her unique way, has tried to restore to me some sense of belonging. I dearly love each and every one of them and am so thankful to God for bringing them into my life. I am glad I was adopted and I deeply loved my adoptive parents, but I am also grateful that I could finally meet the family who gave me life. Uncle Dave and Aunt Marge have proven true the words he once said to me, "Sherrie, there is no 'rejection' in our vocabulary."

When I realized that I had just as much a right to be a member of my birth family as my rejecting birth mother did, a totally unexpected series of blessings came my way. Any of us can make a choice that can be truly life-changing when we realize that our extended family may welcome us with open arms.

Our Choice
To reach out to other birth relatives even if our birth parents or siblings reject us.

This is not easy to do! It takes courage. But remember, we are given the courage at the moment we need it.

How to begin

- *Write a letter.* I believe this is the best way to make initial contact with any birth family member. Make it short and sweet. Be sure and tell them that you want nothing from them, just to meet.

- *Brace yourself for a blowup.* Many of our rejecting birth mothers are emotionally unstable, so we can expect a strong reaction from them whenever we cross into what they consider "their territory." Don't allow fear of what your birth mother might say or do stop you from reaching out to extended family members. Haven't you already given her enough power over your life? Go ahead, follow as you are led.

- *Have someone else answer the phone, if possible.* My birth mother actually had the nerve to have one of her friends call me and tell me "to leave her alone." I wasn't contacting her, I was contacting the rest of my family! If you have a spouse or partner, have them answer the phone whenever possible after sending your letter. Setting healthy boundaries can keep you safe from further abuse.

The next chapter deals with letting go of our birth mother's original decision to send us away. That decision brings a welcome result.

"To err is human, to forgive, divine."

—ALEXANDER POPE

CHAPTER twenty

Letting Go of Our Birth Mother's Original Decision Will Set Us Free

One or two years after my birth mother rejected me, I tried everything I possibly could to bring about reconciliation. I got mad at people who kept saying: "Give her another chance." "Leave the door open." "Turn the other cheek."

Well, I turned the other cheek again and again until I didn't have one left! She would have no part of me...that is, until she finally contacted me to tell me her other daughter had died. She was in a vulnerable spot.

"It's time to let go. It's okay to let go," the nightingale whispered.

Our contact went well in the beginning. I welcomed her with open arms as I'd promised I would do, yet I wouldn't trust her any farther than I could throw a boxcar. During some conversations, I broached the subject of adoption in a very cautious way. I *began* trusting her, from a distance. In fact, she even considered coming for Christmas that year to meet the family. But within nine months of her coming back into my life, she was gone. This time it wasn't her doing, it was mine, for she began lashing out at me once again with venomous statements. After that she began infiltrating my family, telling lies about me.

When my birthday drew near—a trigger point for many adoptees and birth mothers—she became verbally abusive during a phone call with me. If I'd had a tape of the original rejection, this would be a replay of it. She raked me over the coals. But about halfway through her tirade, it dawned on me, *I don't have to take this anymore.* Then I calmly proceeded to tell her that I didn't think our relationship was going to work and that it was time to say goodbye. Up until that time I would have done *anything* to get her to love me. Stand on my head, turn cartwheels. You name it. But finally, I didn't *need* her love. I could let go.

She seemed happy at the prospect and then, after telling me again that she wished she had aborted me, she closed the conversation with "God bless you."

Say what?

I felt like a grand piano had been lifted off my back. I was free at last to move into the future, for I had let go of her original decision to relinquish me as well as her subsequent rejections of me. I felt like the alpine climber who was preparing to ascend a high mountain. His load became extremely heavy and early in the climb he was physically overcome. The guide said that the climber must make a choice, for he was not only hindering his own climb, but also the climb of others to whom he was roped.

He must either give up hope of reaching the top or give up the weights. The question he finally had to answer was, "Do I let go of all these things so that I may gain the summit?"[1]

I am so glad and grateful that I chose to let go of what was hindering my climb to the summit—the need for my birth mother's love. Now, when I tell my story, I say that I love my birth mother, pray for her often, and still consider her my hero for giving me life. Others can't understand how I could possibly feel this way about her after what she has done to me. The reason is that I have forgiven her.

Was it easy? No. It took a long, long time, and I had to see my own need for forgiveness before I could even consider forgiving her. But it is a decision I will never regret.

Cutting ourselves loose

Many of us must face the issue of forgiveness. You may be saying, "No way, Sherrie. You can't possibly be suggesting that you just let her off the hook after all she's put you through!"

Hold tight…I want only what is best for you. You may feel angry with me for even bringing up the subject, as I did when others kept telling me to "turn the other cheek." Believe me, I understand. But may I ever so gently ask if you would be willing to forgive? If not for your birth mother, then for yourself?

Author and speaker Beth Moore vividly illustrates what happens when we aren't willing to forgive. She says it is as if we have the very person we resent roped to our backs. Ironically, we bind ourselves to that which we hate the most.[2]

Now I know for a fact that none of us wants to carry our birth mothers around for life! Some of us, especially those who have been rejected, may hate our birth mothers with a vengeance. But you know what? The rejection probably isn't bothering them a bit. We're the only ones suffering.

Cheri Freeman carried her birth mother on her back for years. At a New Year's Eve service at her church in 1999, the pastor urged individuals to let go of old baggage before going into the new millennium. Cheri went forward, and as her pastor prayed for her, she envisioned her birth mother on a cliff, miles across a deep gorge. "For the first time in my life, there was no string between us, nothing tying me to her," Cheri says:

> I not only felt strong enough to stand, but I felt safe. That's the first time I realized how afraid I had been of her. Suddenly, all the anger, hurt, and bitterness simply disappeared, and I was able to pray for her and to ask for God's blessings upon her for the first time. To me, to be able to sincerely ask for God's blessings upon her is the meaning of forgiveness!

Can you imagine the benefits that would come from being able to cut loose from the person who is causing you so much anguish? You would no longer feel the weight of their pain and shame and no longer have to hear them repeating the same negative words in your ears.

Though forgiveness is a mystery to many, and to others an order from a demanding God, perhaps you had never considered it being for your own good. Knowing now the self-destructive effects of not forgiving, are you warming up to the idea of forgiveness? Are you willing to go on to the next step with me?

Forgiveness

Forgiveness is rarely a one-time event. It's not pretending that a hurt didn't matter or is okay. It's not tolerance. It's not make-believe. It's a process, which I hope this book has helped us journey through.

Author David Augsburger says, "To 'forgive' is, in the English language, an extended, expanded, strengthened form of the verb *to give*. By intensifying the verb we speak of giving at its deepest level, of self-giving, of giving forth and *giving up* deeply held parts of the self."[3]

Considering the true meaning of forgiveness, let's see how it fleshes out in everyday life for fellow adoptees. How did they let go? How did they forgive?

Realizing we can't change the past

Karen says letting go of her birth mother is *accepting* that she was adopted and that she can't change that fact. She says:

> It would have been much easier to "let go" if she had told me, when we met, that she had missed me, wanted to know how I was doing, or any of those things you think a mother separated from her child for twenty years would want to know.

But Karen accepted her birth mother's response—or lack thereof—as well…because she couldn't change it.

Being content with the unknown

This is difficult, to say the least. Dawn Saphir believes that many years ago, when her mother chose adoption, it was a very loving act. She explains that in Korean culture, the reasons for giving children up for adoption are often harsher than what Americans would be able to understand. "I have explored many if not all of those options and have come to terms with the fact that any one of them may have been my birth mother's reasons for giving me up." She has chosen to let go of the details she will never be able to know.

Giving up the "what ifs"

Richard Curtis says his birth mother's decision to give him up had an incredible impact on his life. But long ago he stopped dwelling on the "what ifs" and went ahead with life according to a plan that still is unfolding. "Now I can simply live each day to the fullest with all of the energy, love, and truth that I can put forth."

Being grateful that she tried her best

Teresa Armor is quite sure that her mother wanted to keep her and that she lived with her at least a year before being abandoned outside of an orphanage in Seoul, Korea. She's made peace with whatever situations or factors led her birth mother to realize that she couldn't care for Teresa anymore. She is happy and fulfilled in her life, which might not have happened had her birth mother chosen to keep her.

Derek Jeske is thankful that his birth mother at least made the decision to create an adoption plan for him. He is reminded of this every time he reads about an infant being found dead in a dumpster.

Getting over ourselves

Ron Hilliard's interpretation of being relinquished was that it was mostly about him...something *wrong* with him. Letting go of his birth mother's decision required coming to the place of realizing that the decision wasn't about him, but was about her and whatever was going on in her life. For Ron, letting go of her decision has involved forgiving her, which is an ongoing process.

Uncovering part of the story of his relinquishment has been a part of that process because it has helped him understand some of the circumstances and influences that led to her decision.

Verbalizing his experience and feelings within a safe place and being open to the entire story (not just his own interpretation of what happened) has helped a lot. As Ron has processed this, he has begun to understand that his birth mother's decision might have actually been prompted by love, having his best interests at heart.

For Sharon, letting go and forgiving means "giving up the adoption excuse"—that being adopted is the reason for all of her problems. It means having sympathy for her birth mother, especially at the time of relinquishment.

Depending on your faith

The late Corrie ten Boom had to ask God to make her willing to forgive her Nazi perpetrators. During World War II, she and her family were arrested for concealing Jews in their home in Holland, thrown into a concentration camp at Ravensbruck, and brutally tortured by the guards. Corrie was the only member of her family who survived.

Years later, during a speaking engagement, she mentioned having been in Ravensbruck. Afterward a man came up to shake her hand, and when she looked into his face she remembered him as one of the former Nazi guards who had tortured her. She struggled to move her hand toward him but felt frozen. She told God that there was no way for her to forgive this brutal murderer. Finally she asked God to help her.

She raised her hand, almost mechanically, and recalled, "From my shoulder along my arm and through my hand a current seemed to pass from me to him, while into my heart sprang a love for this stranger that almost overwhelmed me."[4]

Now, that's miraculous!

I feel like I experienced my own miracle after saying goodbye to my birth mother for the last time. This is the poem I wrote to "commemorate" that letting-go event.

Letting Go

Letting go
  How can it be?
  Of she who was supposed to care for me?
Why did she do it?
  I'll never know
  But someday the other side of the tapestry will show.
Not knowing she loves me
  Or that she even cares
  Has set me on a path filled with pain and snares.
But now the ifs and what-might-have-beens have to go
  No matter the process,
  No matter how slow.
I'm letting go of her original choice
  I'm no longer bound
  I'm at peace and can finally rejoice.

I hope you're thinking at least a little differently about the issues of letting go and forgiving than you were before you began reading this chapter. Perhaps you are ready to make a life-transforming choice.

Our Choice
To move toward forgiveness.

Author C.S. Lewis tells a story about a ghost arriving at heaven with a lizard on his lapel. Apparently this lizard was the center of the ghost's life—they were intimate friends. The ghost had been preoccupied with the lizard for years. The truth of the matter, however, was that the lizard was demanding, burdened the ghost with fatigue, and left scales all over his clothes. Nonetheless, the lizard continued to live there with the ghost's permission.

On the day the ghost arrived at heaven's gate the gatekeeper said, "You must kill that lizard. No lizards are allowed in heaven."

How could he possibly part with his lizard? Yet he wanted heaven so much.

Finally the ghost tore the lizard from his body and threw it to the ground.

The lizard cried pitifully and then died…but then an amazing thing happened. The dead lizard transformed into a beautiful horse that carried the ghost into heaven in triumph.[5]

This is exactly what happened to me and many fellow adoptees when we got rid of the lizard of resentment and hatred on our lapels.

How to begin

- *Read some good books on forgiveness.* David Augsburger's book *The Freedom of Forgiveness* is a good place to start.

- *Make a drawing.* Draw a picture of you with your rejecting birth mother tied to your back. Include quotes about what you may be saying as you carry her around in everyday life. Then make a second drawing of cutting her free.

- *List all the freedoms you are about to enjoy.*

We've jumped one of the highest hurdles and now we're ready for the rest of our lives. That's what we'll talk about next.

We are products of our past, but we don't have to be prisoners of it.

—RICK WARREN

CHAPTER twenty-one

We *Can* Discover Our Life Purpose

A few years ago, Bob and I were being trained as life coaches. One break-out session was especially appealing to me—"How to Help Others Find Their Life Purpose."

When the two leaders asked for a volunteer to come up front and be their "guinea pig client" to demonstrate how to find their life purpose, I raised my hand. I already knew what my life purpose and passion was. This would be a piece of cake!

Standing between the two leaders and in front of at least 50 people, they asked, "What is your passion?"

"Orphans," I said, with confidence.

Suddenly, I was overcome with emotion. Please understand this is not normal behavior for me. I was wearing my "I have it all together adoptee mask," after all! But I couldn't stop the tears. I turned my back to the crowd, putting my hands over quivering lips.

"This is a normal reaction when people find their passion," the coaches said. "Often, the passion hits deep chords and tears come, very unexpectedly."

After I turned around, they asked, "And, what happened in your life that you feel a passion for orphans?"

"I was an orphan," I whispered.

Then, they asked, "And, what do you want to do with this passion?"

With a hoarse voice, I answered, "I want to hold each one of them and tell them that they're not forgotten."

The teaching they gave afterwards has been emblazoned on my heart as I have taken steps to find my life purpose.

Past hurts may lead to your life purpose

This is a key concept coaches use to help people find their life purpose. Ask yourself the same thing I was asked by the coaches:

- What have been some of the greatest hurts from your past?

- What set of people do you feel drawn to help? Maybe you get teary-eyed whenever you hear others mention them.

It is my belief that our dreams begin as adopted children. I wanted to be a great ice skater, like Sonje Henne. I thought I was really good and I knew I could do it.

You were born for greatness

What about you? What great things did you aspire to as a child? Don't be embarrassed.

So, we have our childhood dreams, but when we hit the "adoptee rite of passage," our dreams may die, along with any sense of self-confidence or worth. Like a little grain of wheat that's been pounded on the threshing floor and then placed in the ground to multiply, it's been too dark, too long, for us to perhaps even remember those dreams.

That's okay. Dreams must die before they can really live, and that's what happened during your "rite of passage" into this upcoming wonderful part of life.

What about now? If cost were no object, if energy or circumstances were not objects, what would you l-o-v-e to do in life? Don't be bashful.

In the years ahead, you will find yourself at many crossroads of life. Which way should you go? You could go many ways, you can do multiple things, but which is the absolute *best* way to turn?

A life-defining principle for decision making

A mentor once taught me a life-defining principle for making choices at crossroads. She said: "Ask yourself what you are the *most uniquely* qualified for." In other words:

- Which of the two options could anyone do?

- Which of the two could only you do?

At one of my personal crossroads, I had just been accepted into a Master's program for counseling. It was an honor to be chosen as one of ten.

However, another dream was brewing inside me. I dreamed of writing material for fellow adoptees that would encourage them on every level.

So, one door was wide open, but the other was a dream. Long story short, I quit the Master's program and began writing *Jewels Adoption News*, way back in 1994, when hard copies were the only form of communication. Readership increased by 500 percent the first year, and it was then that I knew I'd taken the right path. In addition, it was so incredibly fulfilling!

Growth may come gradually

I'm in my sixth decade of life now, and looking back, it is clear that confidence in finding my life purpose came slowly. You may feel the same…not sure of where you should be right now? That's okay, my friend. Just keep asking yourself those key questions my mentor taught me, and you'll look back someday and know you were on the right path all along. There are some advantages to age!

While you're making your decisions, be sure to never say never! I always said, "I will never do public speaking," but look how my life has unfolded. Don't be afraid to get out of your comfort zone and take a risk. You may be surprised…you may actually end up enjoying what you vowed you'd never do.

Discover your strengths through coaching

If possible, find a good coach. Bob and I were trained to be Strengths Coaches by Insights International, Inc.

In helping people find their strengths, this is the process:

- The individual takes a personal inventory.

- We read the inventory results in general terms and ask them to underline words and phrases that resonate as their personality.

- Then we read a more specific inventory, listing their strengths and weaknesses, and ask them to do the same.

- Next, we show them 10–15 of their personal characteristics that make them valuable as a team member. Again, they underline what resonates.

- Then they are shown a checklist for communicating (the do's and don'ts of communicating effectively.

- The ideal environment is then described, along with keys to leading.[1]

So, my friend, you have so much to look forward to. Even though your knees may shake and you might feel terribly green, go for that dream. Remember, you were made for it!

Our Choice
To choose the life path we are most uniquely qualified for.

How to begin

- *Identify your greatest hurt in life.* Write it, journal it, feel it, remember it.

- *Coach yourself!* Did you know that many times our life purpose comes from our deepest life hurts?

- *Search the internet for free coaching tools.* You can probably learn a lot for free!

A shared pain is no longer paralyzing but mobilizing, when understood as a way to liberation.

—HENRI J. M. NOUWEN

——— CHAPTER twenty-two

We Can Help Others Find Their Way

Having a heart for others who are hurting is strong evidence that healing and redemption have occurred in our lives. If we attend support groups, we now do so not only to find healing for ourselves, but also to come alongside others who are struggling. If we give seminars and workshops, we do so not to build our egos and find a sense of identity, but to point out the road of restoration to those who have yet to find it. We long to reach out and help others discover the riches that we have found. The very pain we spent so long running from becomes our ticket into the fellowship of wounded healers.

I love Henri Nouwen's concept of the "wounded healer" because that is what I believe we can become after working through our own pain. Wounded healers are uniquely equipped to listen to and even enter into the pain of others without discomfort or fear.[1]

I remember my therapist saying, "I can go to the mat with you." What she meant is that she could go into the pain with me and not abandon me out of fear because she had not done her own emotional work. She proved that true again and again. For example, when I got in touch with my anger, she said, "Scream, Sherrie. Just scream!" Well, I was too self-conscious to do so, so she started and I joined in! Up until then I had been alone in my anger. I soon realized that I had a friend in the fire with me. I was no longer alone. What comfort!

Nouwen explains that we can offer hurting people a special kind of "hospitality" by giving them a safe, friendly, empty space where they can be whatever they want to be and find their souls.[2]

Great things about wounded healers

From the lives of wounded healers flow blessings desperately needed by those who are still suffering.

An ability to empathize with others

The primary task of a wounded healer, Nouwen explains, is not to take away pain but to deepen it to a level where it can be shared. When someone comes to a wounded healer with his loneliness, he can only expect that his loneliness will be understood and felt, so that he no longer has to run away from it, but accept it as an expression of his basic human condition.[3]

The wounded healer isn't one who has his or her act together, but rather, one who is willing to share the burden of personal pain with others. Because of Frieda Moore's experiences, she can empathize with others and listen with an unguarded and loving heart. She knows full well what it's like to not belong, to be rejected, and to wander aimlessly in life. Because she has learned that she is not the only one to suffer such experiences, she feels free to share her life with others and to be the kind of "safe" person we all need.

Dawn Saphir doesn't mind sharing her pain, joys, failures, and triumphs because as an adoptee from Korea her life has so often been an open book, whether or not she wanted it to be. Because she has often been the subject of curiosity, she has learned to share her story over and over again. Today she participates in panel discussions and talks to prospective adoptive parents about some of her experiences growing up. As she tries to offer them insight into what their experiences might be with their adoptive children, it is a blessing for her and for them.

Cheri Manternach's adoption experience has helped her be supportive of girls who relinquished their babies for adoption when they weren't sure what they should do. It's also helped her be supportive of friends who have adopted.

Because Sheila Rounds has been willing to talk about her adoption experience, others have realized they are not alone. "When talking to people I refer to Mom as my birth mom. That alone attracts attention. I deal very well with people who feel loneliness or shame or are shy, because as an adoptee I have felt all of these things."

Karen says she has become the kind of person people come to for an ear, or for a friend. Being adopted has created within her an almost uncanny understanding of people and their feelings, of how things aren't always what they appear to be. She doesn't think she could do that without the experiences adoption has brought her.

Sandy Garrett says she has actually become eager to talk to folks about adoption...and reunion. She has a better understanding of birth mothers and all the emotional issues associated with their decisions to relinquish their children for adoption. She finds herself able to talk to all members of the adoption triad—adoptive parents, adoptees, and birth mothers—whether to give advice or just a shoulder. To Sandy, that is a true blessing. She says she would never be able to understand anyone in the triad if she had not been through all the ups and downs of adoption.

Jody Moreen says:

> A passion began to grow within me to be available to encourage others in their adoption journeys. I have been involved in two adoption newsletter publications, have facilitated adoption support groups, and recently began leading an adoption Bible study for the adoption triad. I find it fascinating that my adoptee status has led me to help others touched by adoption. It is wonderful to find that even your most painful life experience can equip you to reach out to others!

The capacity to inspire others

"I believe I can present people with a positive example of how well adoption can work out," says Rick Ennis. "Despite difficulties physically and emotionally that would make many parents shy away from accepting a child like me for adoption at age three, I am a poster-child/adult of the power of nurture versus nature."

Thanks to Rick's many blessings, he feels motivated to speak to groups touched by adoption, and to share with them that all of their hard work is worth it. He's stumbled into doing adoption presentations, originally intending to share professional knowledge. But along the way he noticed that his story was inspiring people in the audience, not because of his knowledge, but because of the many obstacles he's been able to overcome. "While it is not my intention to inspire by 'tooting my horn,'" Rick says, "it is a blessing to have a special story to share, and it is a pleasure to share that I am now proud to have been adopted. After all, I've been twice loved and doubly blessed!"

Bob Blanchard, one of the list owners of the Adoptees Internet Mailing List (AIML), the largest adoptee support group on the internet, says, "I've had the privilege of helping thousands of adoptees through the many issues adoption brings into our lives. I've also helped countless others with their searches for their birth families. Many have resulted in life-changing reunions."

A heart for serving

Ron Hilliard says:

> I am who I am today because of being relinquished and adopted. I believe that God was involved in the process and I am where I am, and who I am, as a result. If I had not been relinquished and adopted I would be a very different person, and while I might be serving God, it wouldn't be in the place where I am today.

The life accounts of these, my fellow adoptees, reminds me of a story about two men who were climbing different trails high in the mountains. After a while, they came to a place where their paths met. It was such a narrow ledge that only one person could get past. Their dilemma seemed impossible to resolve—there was no way both of them could make it.

It was then that one climber lay down and let the other walk over him. The other climber could subsequently go on to new heights. Neither man was left behind.[4]

That is what we are accomplishing when we serve as wounded healers. The painful repercussions of adoption loss won't completely dissipate for any of us, but they can become welcoming invitations for others to deal with their own issues and find community. And so, what is our concluding choice?

Our Choice

To be real and authentic.

From all that has been shared by fellow adoptees in this book, it is clear to me, and I hope to you, that a painful beginning can be transformed into something of beauty. Broken wings can mend and learn to fly.

How to begin

- *Start a support group.* There are several for free at my site: www.SherrieEldridge.com.

- *Write an email to me.* I would love to hear from you! My address is sherriesheartlanguage@gmail.com.

I wish for you, dear readers, hearts that marvel at the incredible lessons that adoption can teach. Wherever you are in your process is where you're supposed to be. Milk it for all it's worth! Search out safe people. Embrace the pain. Listen to the echoes of loss, and turn over every stone possible in coming to peace with your past. Start enjoying friendships with fellow adoptees, if you haven't already.

And as you do all of this, know that I am your number one cheerleader, urging you on to become all that you were created to be.

It's strange as I write these last words; my eyes are welling with tears. I guess it's because I'm saying goodbye, and you know how we adoptees feel about goodbyes!

RESOURCES FOR ADOPTEES

Books

Adoptees Come of Age. Ronald J. Nydam. Westminster John Knox Press, 1999

Adopting the Hurt Child: Hope for Families with Special-Needs Kids—A Guide for Parents and Professionals. Gregory C. Keck and Regina M. Kupecky. Piñon Press, 1998

Adoption and the Family System. Miriam Reitz and Ken Watson. Guilford Press, 1991

Adoption Healing...A Path to Recovery. Joe Soll. Liturgical Press, 2000

Adoption Reunion Survival Guide: Preparing Yourself for the Search, Reunion, and Beyond. Julie Jarrell Bailey, Lynn N. Giddens, New Harbinger Publishers, 2001

A Koala for Katie (for ages 9–12). Jonathan London and Cynthia Jabar. Albert Whitman & Company, 1977

A Man and His Mother: An Adopted Son's Search. Tim Green. HarperCollins Publishers, 1997

Ambiguous Loss. Pauline Boss. Harvard University Press, 2000

cAndrew, You Died Too Soon. Corrine Chilstrom. Augsburg Press, 1993

Being Adopted: The Lifelong Search for Self. David M. Brodzinsky, and Marshall D. Schechter, Doubleday, 1992

Birth Bond: Reunions Between Birthparents and Adoptees—What Happens After. Judith S. Gediman and Linda P. Brown. New Horizon Press, 1989

Boundaries: When to Say Yes and When to Say No to Take Control of Your Life. Henry Cloud and John Townsend. Zondervan, 1992

Destiny and Deliverance: Spiritual Insights from the Life of Moses. Philip Yancey, Max Lucado, John C. Maxwell, Jack Hayford, Joni Bareckson Tada, Tommi Barnett, Kenneth Boa, Thelma Wells. Thomas Nelson, 1998

Facilitating Developmental Attachment: The Road to Emotional Recovery and Behavior Change in Foster and Adopted Children. Daniel A. Hughes. Jason Aronson Inc., 1997

Forgive and Forget: Healing the Hurts We Don't Deserve. Lewis B. Smedes. HarperCollins Publishers, 1984

Good Grief Rituals. Elaine Child-Gowell. Station Hill Press, 1992

Growing Up Again: Parenting Ourselves, Parenting Our Children. Jean Illsley Clarke and Connie Dawson, Hazelden Informational Education, 1998

I Hope You Have a Good Life: A True Story of Love, Loss, and Redemption. Campbell Armstrong. Crown Publishers, 2000

Journeys After Adoption: Understanding Lifelong Issues. Jayne E. Schooler and Betsie Norris. Bergin and Garvey, 2002

Journey of the Adopted Self: A Quest for Wholeness. Betty Jean Lifton. HarperCollins Publishers, 1994

Life Is Goodbye, Life Is Hello: Grieving Well Through All Kinds of Losses. Alla Renee Bozarth. Hazelden Informational Education, 1994

Lost and Found: The Adoption Experience. Betty Jean Lifton. Harper Collins, 1988

Loved by Choice: True Stories that Celebrate Adoption. Susan E. Horner and Kelly Fordyce Martindale. Fleming H. Revell Company, 2002

May the Circle Be Unbroken. Lynn C. Franklin with Elizabeth Ferber. Harmony Books, 1998

Moses, Great Lives Series—Volume 4. Charles R. Swindoll. Word Publishing, 1999

Painful Lessons, Loving Bonds: The Heart of Open Adoption. Marcy Wineman Axness. Self-published booklet. Order through: axness@earthlink.net

Parenting the Hurt Child: Helping Adoptive Families Heal and Grow. Gregory C. Keck and Regina M. Kupecky. Piñon Press, 2002

Patterns of Relating: An Adult Attachment Perspective. Malcolm L. West and Adrienne E. Sheldon-Keller. Guilford Press, 1994

Reunion: A Year in Letters Between a Birthmother and the Daughter She Couldn't Keep. Katie Hern and Ellen McGarry Carlson. Seal Press, 1999

Search: A Handbook for Adoptees and Birth Parents. Jayne Askin. Oryx Press, 1998

Secret Thoughts of an Adoptive Mother. Jana Wolff. Vista Communications, 1999

Stones of Fire. Isobel Kuhn. OMF, Singapore, 1989. Order directly from: 404 South Church Street, Robesonia, PA 19551

Telling the Truth to Your Adopted Child: Making Sense of the Past. Jayne E. Schooler and Betsy E. Keefer. Bergin and Garvey, 2000

The Adoption Reunion Survival Guide: Preparing Yourself for the Search. Julie Jarrell Bailey and Lynn N. Giddens, New Harbinger Publication Inc., 2001

The Adoption Triangle: The Effects of the Sealed Record on Adoptees, Birth Parents, and Adoptive Parents. Arthur D. Sorosky. Anchor Press (out of print)

The Crippled Lamb (children's book, but also lovely for adults). Max Lucado. Word Publishing, 1994

The Family of Adoption. Joyce Maguire Pavao. Beacon Press, 1999

The Gift Nobody Wants: The Inspiring Story of a Surgeon Who Discovers Why We Hurt and What We Can Do About It. Paul Brand with Philip Yancey. HarperCollins Publishers, 1995

The Freedom of Forgiveness. David Augsburger. Moody Press, 1988

The Message: The Bible in Contemporary Language. Eugene H. Peterson. NavPress, 2002

The Other Mother: A Woman's Love for the Child She Gave Up for Adoption. Carol Schaefer. Soho Press, 1992

The Primal Wound: Understanding the Adopted Child. Nancy Verrier. Gateway Press, Inc., 1994

The Psychology of Adoption. David M. Brodzinsky, and Marshall D. Schechter, Oxford University Press, 1990

The Whole Life Adoption Book: Realistic Advice for Building a Healthy Adoptive Family. Jayne E. Schooler. NavPress, 1993

Twice Born: Memoirs of an Adopted Daughter. Betty Jean Lifton. McGraw-Hill, 1975

What Is Written On the Heart…Primal Issues in Adoption. Marcy Wineman Axness. Order through: axness@earthlink.net

When to Forgive. Mona Gustafson Affinito. New Harbinger Publishing, 1999

Whose Child? An Adoptee's Healing Journey from Relinquishment Through Reunion…and Beyond. Kasey Hamner. Triad Publishing, 2000

W.I.S.E-Up® Powerbook. Marilyn Schoettle. CASE, 2000

Worthy to Be Found. Deanna Doss Shrodes. Entourage Publishing, 2014

Websites

www.adoption.com

Founded in 1982, the Independent Adoption Center has successfully finalized more than 2000 adoptions in thirty-five states and is fully licensed in the states of California, Indiana, Georgia, and North Carolina. As a nonprofit organization, its mission is to make open adoption a viable and accessible alternative to untimely pregnancy throughout the US by providing professional, licensed, comprehensive educational and counseling-centered services to birth parents, adopting parents, and adoptees nationwide.

www.adoption.org
This organization has been in existence since 1994 and offers everything from information on DNA testing to life books and jewelry.

www.AdoptionBoards.com
This site offers more than 600 adoption-related message boards.

www.americanadoptioncongress.org
The American Adoption Congress (AAC) is composed of individuals, families, and organizations committed to adoption reform. Through education and advocacy, it promotes honesty, openness, and respect for family connections in adoption and foster care.

www.adoptioncrossroads.org
This is the site of the Council for Equal Rights in Adoption (CERA), an organization dedicated to the preservation and reunification of families "with liberty and justice for all." It is the largest search and support network in the world for adoptees and birth parents.

www.adoptionregistry.com
This site is the internet's largest reunion registry dedicated exclusively to adoption.

www.adoptionsupport.org/kids
The Center for Adoption Support and Education, Inc. is an incredible, multi-faceted organization offering all kinds of services for kids and parents. The center includes a clinical team of social workers, psychologists, psychiatrists, and educators with demonstrated expertise to offer post-adoption counseling. You can order your *W.I.S.E-Up° Powerbook* at this site.

www.aiml.org
The Adoptees Internet Mailing List (AIML) is a place where adoptees can gather for advice in conducting a search and/or discussions of our varied reunion outcomes. AIML also encourages discussions of social, media, and legal issues related to adoption.

www.attach.org
The Association for Treatment and Training in the Attachment of Children (ATTACh) is an international coalition of parents, professionals, and others working to increase awareness about attachment and its critical importance to human development.

www.calib.com/naic
The National Adoption Information Clearinghouse (NAIC) provides a comprehensive resource, including statistics, laws, databases, and publications. A five-page packet of free information for your support groups about adoption, etc. is sent upon request.

www.chosenchildren.org
This organization offers financial help to adoptees who want to reunite but lack the funding needed.

www.Christianadoptions.com
This is a biblically based site that offers daily adoption-related devotionals and a plethora of articles for those touched by adoption.

www.geocites.com/brkwlsurvivors
This site provides a safe place for adoptees who have experienced rejection to bare their souls without judgment.

www.tapestrybooks.com
Complete catalogue of adoption books. Request a free catalogue at info@ tapestrybooks.com.

www.twpcc.org
Spiritual Link's mission is to affirm one's need for his or her own "wilderness experience" and the search for meaning—a spiritual connection. A great place to come for pastoral care.

Therapeutic resources

Twelve Steps for Adopted Teens!
Sherrie co-authored this with a teen who has worked through adoption issues and transparently shares her heart. It is biblically based and suitable for parents/ teens, teen support groups, counselors/clients.

Twenty Things Adopted Kids Wish Their Adoptive Parents Knew: A Study Guide
Companion study guide to *Twenty Things Adopted Kids Wish Their Adoptive Parents Knew*, this includes the biblical perspective not included in the book.

Under His Wings: Creating a Safe Place to Talk about Adoption
Spanish Edition—free at SherrieEldridge.com
Takes the adoptee on an imaginary search for their birth mother by writing letters TO and FROM her. Based on the life of Moses, it is suitable for individual, client/counselor, or support group use.

NOTES

Chapter One

1. Adapted from Isaiah 49:15-16, NIV.

Chapter Two

1. J. I. Rodale, *The Synonym Finder* (Emmaus, PA: Rodale Press, 1978), p. 1318.
2. Judith Viorst, *Imperfect Control: Our Lifelong Struggles with Power and Surrender* (New York, NY: Simon & Schuster, 1998), p. 16.
3. Rosamund Stone Zander and Benjamin Zander, *The Art of Possibility: Transforming Professional and Personal Life* (Boston, MA.: Harvard Business School Press, 2000), pp. 9–10.
4. Spencer Johnson, *One Minute for Yourself: A Simple Strategy for a Better Life* (New York, NY: Quill-William Morrow, 1991), p. 26.
5. Jack Hayford, *Destiny and Deliverance: Spiritual Insights from the Life of Moses* (Nashville, TN: Thomas Nelson Publishers), p. 41.

Chapter Three

1. John Bowlby, as quoted by Bob Mullan in *Are Mothers Really Necessary?* (New York, NY: Weidenfield and Nicholson, 1987), p. 71.
2. Peter Nathananielsz, *The Prenatal Prescription* (New York, NY: HarperCollins Publishers, 2001), p. 3.

3. Thomas Verny, *The Secret Life of the Unborn Child* (New York, NY: Dell Publishing, 1981), p. 78.
4. Judith Viorst, *Necessary Losses* (New York, NY: Simon & Schuster, 1986), pp. 22–23.
5. Arthur Janov, *The New Primal Scream* (Wilmington, DE: Enterprise Publishing, Inc., 1991), pp. 26–27.
6. Mary Watkins and Susan Fisher, *Talking with Young Children about Adoption* (New Haven, CT and London: Yale University Press), p. 226.
7. Louise Kaplan, as quoted by Daniel A. Hughes, in *Facilitating Developmental Attachment* (North Bergen, NJ and London: Jason Aronson Inc., 1997), pp. 14, 15, 20.
8. Penny Callan Partridge, *Pandora's Hope* (Amherst, MA: Self-published, 1997). Used with permission.

Chapter Four

1. Exodus 2:6, NIV.
2. *New American Exhaustive Concordance of the Bible*, p. 1948.
3. Gregory C. Keck, as quoted in an interview by Sherrie Eldridge, 2001.
4. J. I. Rodale, *The Synonym Finder* (Emmaus, PA: Rodale Press, 1978), p. 1319.
5. Nancy Verrier, *The Primal Wound* (Baltimore, MD: Gateway Press, 1994), p. 77.
6. John and Paula Sanford, *Healing the Wounded Spirit* (South Plainfield, NJ: Bridge Publishing, Inc., 1985), p. 30.
7. Selma Fraiberg, *Every Child's Birthright: In Defense of Mothering* (New York, NY: Bantam Books, 1997), p. 72.
8. Gregory C. Keck, as quoted in an interview by Sherrie Eldridge, 2001.
9. David M. Brodzinsky and Marshall D. Schechter, *The Psychology of Adoption* (New York, NY and Oxford: Oxford University Press, 1990), pp. 45–46.
10. From *Ghost at Heart's Edge*, edited by Susan Ito and Tina Cervin ©1999. Published by North Atlantic Books. Reprinted by permission of the publisher.
11. Corrine Chilstrom, *Andrew, You Died Too Soon* (Minneapolis, MS: Augsburg Fortress, 1993), p. 17.

Chapter Six

1. David M. Brodzinsky and Marshall D. Schechter, *The Psychology of Adoption* (New York, NY, and Oxford: Oxford University Press, 1990), p. 85.
2. J. I. Rodale, *The Synonym Finder* (Emmaus, PA: Rodale Press, 1978), p. 740.

3. Marilyn Schoettle, *The WISE-UP® Powerbook* (Silver Spring, MD.: The Center for Adoption Support and Education, Inc., 2000), pp. 16–19. Contact CASE (11120 New Hampshire Ave., Suite 205, Silver Spring, MD 20904) at their website: www.adoptionsupport.org. Used by permission.

Chapter Seven

1. David M. Brodzinsky and Marshall D. Schechter, *The Psychology of Adoption* (New York, NY and Oxford: Oxford University Press, 1990), p. 26.
2. http://web.cortland.edu/andersmd/erik/welcome.html, October 13, 2014.
3. Malcolm L. West and Adrienne E. Sheldon-Keller, *Patterns of Relating: An Adult Attachment Perspective* (New York, NY and London: The Guilford Press, 1994), p. 83.
4. Lillian Glass, *Toxic People: 10 Ways of Dealing with People Who Make Your Life Miserable* (New York, NY: St Martin's Griffin, 1997), p. 55.
5. David Augsburger, *Caring Enough to Hear and Be Heard* (Ventura, CA: Regal Books, 1982), p. 72. Used by permission.
6. Ibid., p. 83. Used by permission.

Chapter Eight

1. Ephesians 4:26, MSG.
2. Carol Komissaroff, *Quest: The Newsletter of KinQuest, Inc.*, Vol. IV, No. 2, Issue #14, Autumn, 1992.
3. Romans 12:19, MSG.
4. 1 Peter 2:20, NIV.

Chapter Nine

1. 2 Corinthians 12:1–10.
2. Institute in Basic Life Conflicts, Inc., *Character Sketches—Volume One* (Chicago, IL: Rand McNally & Co., 1979), pp. 179–180. Used by permission of the Institute in Basic Life Conflicts, Inc.

Chapter Ten

1. Patrick Thomas Malone, and Thomas Patrick Malone, *The Art of Intimacy* (New York, NY: Simon & Schuster, 1992), p. 19.
2. N. Bohman and A. L. von Knorring, "Psychiatric Illness Among Adults Adopted As Infants," *Acta Paediatrica Scandinavica 60*, pp. 106–112.

3. Arthur Janov, *The New Primal Scream* (Wilmington, DE: Enterprise Publishing, Inc., 1991), p. 26.

Chapter Eleven

1. Joyce Maguire Pavao, as quoted by Sherrie Eldridge in *Jewel Among Jewels Adoption News* (Indianapolis, IN.: Jewel Among Jewels Adoption Network, Inc., Summer 1997), p. 7.
2. Ibid.

Chapter Twelve

1. David M. Brodzinsky and Marshall D. Schechter, *The Psychology of Adoption* (New York, NY and Oxford: Oxford University Press, 1990), p. 87.
2. David M. Brodzinsky, Marshall D. Schechter, and Robin Marantz Henig, *Being Adopted: The Lifelong Search for Self* (New York, NY: Doubleday, 1992), p. 79.
3. *The Random House College Dictionary*, Revised Edition (New York, NY: Random House, Inc., 1975), p. 360.
4. Paul Brand and Phillip Yancey, *The Gift Nobody Wants: The Inspiring Story of a Surgeon Who Discovers Why We Hurt and What We Can Do About It* (New York, NY: HarperCollins, 1995), p. 16.
5. 1 John 1:3, NIV
6. 1 John 1:8-9, MSG
7. Exodus 4:14, NIV
8. John 8:32, NIV

Chapter Fourteen

1. J. I. Rodale, *The Synonym Finder* (Emmaus, PA.: Rodale Press, 1978), p. 685
2. 1 Corinthians 13:6-7, MSG.
3. 1 Corinthians 13:11-12, MSG.

Chapter Fifteen

1. Isaiah 30:21, NIV.

Chapter Sixteen

1. Jayne Askin, *Search* (Phoenix, AZ: Oryx Press, 1998), p. 12.
2. Corrie ten Boom, *Tramp for the Lord* (Old Tappan, NJ: Revell, 1974), pp. 53–54.

Chapter Seventeen

1. Jayne Askin, *Search* (Phoenix, AZ: Oryx Press, 1998), pp. 1–2.
2. Eleanor Doan, *Speaker's Sourcebook* (Grand Rapids, MI.: Zondervan Publishing House, 1960).
3. Dr. Paul Brand with Philip Yancey, *The Gift Nobody Wants* (New York, NY: HarperCollins Publishers, Inc., 1993), pp. 83–84.

Chapter Eighteen

1. *The Random House College Dictionary*, Revised Edition (New York, NY: Random House, Inc., 1975), p. 1113.
2. Ron Nydam, "Doing Rejection" (Indianapolis, IN: *Jewel Among Jewels Adoption News*, Winter 1999), p. 4.
3. *Our Daily Bread*, as quoted by Robert J. Morgan in *Nelson's Complete Book of Stories, Illustrations, and Quotes* (Nashville, TN: Thomas Nelson Publishers, 2000), p. 298.

Chapter Twenty

1. Eleanor Doan, *Speaker's Sourcebook* (Grand Rapids, MI.: Zondervan Publishing House, 1960).
2. Beth Moore, *Living Beyond Yourself* (Nashville: LifeWay Press, 1998), p. 120.
3. David Augsburger, *The Freedom of Forgiveness* (Chicago, IL: Moody Press, 1988), p. 46.
4. Corrie ten Boom, *Tramp for the Lord* (Old Tappan, N.J.: Revell, 1974).
5. www.pastor2youth.com/Illustrations/L/lust.html.

Chapter Twenty-one

1. Bob Eldridge, Ministry Insights Certified Coach, Personal interview, 2014

Chapter Twenty-two

1. Henri J. M. Nouwen, *The Wounded Healer* (New York, NY, London, Toronto, Sydney and Auckland: Image Books-Doubleday, 1990), pp. 92–93.
2. Ibid., pp. 92–93.
3. Ibid., p. 92.
4. Eleanor Doan, *Speaker's Sourcebook* (Grand Rapids, MI.: Zondervan Publishing House, 1960).

ABOUT THE AUTHOR

A twice-reunited adoptee, Sherrie Eldridge is a straight-shooting, transparent, and compassionate author, speaker, blogger, and trainer in the field of adoption. Her books are research-based, yet woven within are poignant messages pounded out on the anvil of her own adoptee heart. This is what makes Sherrie unique! One adoptive parent said she had a beautiful heart because she had the courage to tell him what his daughter might experience.

Her first book, *Twenty Things Adoptive Parents Need to Succeed*, is required reading by many adoption agencies and universities. She has also authored four other books. Sherrie helps readers understand the adopted child's perspective and teaches parents how to "talk adoption" effectively.

Sherrie has been married to Bob Eldridge for forty-nine years. They have two married daughters and six grandchildren. For more information, see: http://SherrieEldridge.com.

Other books by Sherrie Eldridge:

Twenty Things Adopted Kids Wish Their Adoptive Parents Knew...Daily Devotions for Birth and Adoptive Parents (New Hope Publishers, release: August, 2015)

Forever Fingerprints: An Amazing Discovery for Adopted Children (2007 EMK Press, 2014 Jessica Kingsley Publishers)

20 Things Adoptive Parents Need to Succeed (2009, Random House)

Questions Adoptees Are Asking (NavPress, 2009)

20 Things Adopted Kids Wish Their Adoptive Parents Knew (Random House, 1999)